HISTORY CORNER

The Whistler Engineers

Silvio A. Bedini

Among the list of America's most notable civil engineers must be included George Washington Whistler (1800-1849). In 1814, he was appointed to the U. S. Military Academy, where he proved to be an excellent draftsman. Graduating in 1819 with a commission as a second lieutenant in artillery, he was assigned topographical duty.

In 1828, young Whistler assisted in the location and construction of the Baltimore & Ohio Railroad, then was sent to England to study the British railroad system. In the next several years he was assigned to locate the Baltimore & Susquehanna Railroad, then the Paterson & Hudson Railroad and the Boston & Providence Railroad. Resigning from the Army in 1833, Whistler joined the Proprietors of Locks and Canals at Lowell, Massachusetts as engineer and director of the machine shop that produced locomotives.

Four years later, he resumed supervision of the Providence and Stonington Railroad. Between 1840 and 1842, as chief engineer of the Western Railroad of Massachusetts, he located the section between Springfield through the Berkshires, a most difficult problem. One of Whistler's greatest achievements, it attracted the attention of Russian officials visiting the United States to inspect this country's railroad systems, and he was invited by the Czar to become consulting engineer for a double-track railroad projected between St. Petersburg and Moscow.

Decorated by the Czar

The 420-mile rail line was begun in 1844 and completed in 1850, three years ahead of schedule. The rolling stock and other machinery were produced in Russia by an American firm under Whistler's general direction. At the same time he supervised the construction of forts and docks at Cronstadt, and the iron bridge over the Neva River. In 1847, he was decorated by the Czar.

Before the railroad was completed, Whistler became ill with Asian cholera and died in St. Petersburg after a long illness. His remains were returned to the United States and buried in Stonington, Connecticut. He was survived by a daughter and two sons from his first marriage, and by five sons from his second.

One of his sons, George William, was a railroad engineer and continued his father's work in Russia until his own death in 1869.

James Abbot McNeill Whistler (1834-1903) was one of George W. Whistler's sons by his second marriage. Of delicate health from birth, he was already making pencil drawings at the age of four. Although he demonstrated unusual artistic ability, in 1851 his widowed mother arranged for him to enter the U. S. Military Academy when he was barely 17. He remained at the Academy for three years, but was dismissed by Colonel Robert E. Lee, "after my little difference with the Professor of Chemistry...who would not agree with me that silicon was a gas, but declared that it was a metal, and as we could come to no agreement in the matter, it was suggested—all in the most courteous and correct West Point way—that perhaps I had better leave the Academy." He is later reported to have said that, "had silicon been a gas instead of whatever it is, I would have been a major general today, but it may not have been my game."

Loitering in the Drafting Room

After his dismissal, Whistler spent some time in Baltimore, where his brother George was a partner and superintendent in the Winans Locomotive Works. Although repeatedly refusing employment at the Works, Whistler loitered for a time in the Works's drafting rooms, drawing and working out effects which served as training for his later work. Leaving Baltimore a short time later, he went to Washington, hoping to negotiate reinstatement at the Academy. He was refused on the basis that he was too young, but later he was offered the possibility of employment in the U.S. Coast and Geodetic Survey in Washington.

Whistler contacted Captain Benham of the Survey, and on November 7, 1854, six months after he had left West Point, he accepted a position as draftsman of maps. His salary was $1.50 a day, which he later admitted was excessive, considering his poor attendance record.

Whistler was assigned to copy maps, which consisted of rendering a loose drawing upon a copper plate with perfect accuracy. The Survey clerks worked in a great musty barn of a room, filled with row upon row of slant-topped wooden desks at which the draftsmen, seated on high stools, toiled through endless hours. There was nothing that appealed to him in the routine of an office, but he did what he had to do, although without enthusiasm. The records show that he worked six and one half days in January and five and three-fourths days in February. He usually arrived late, but he always claimed the problem was not that he was late but that the office opened too early.

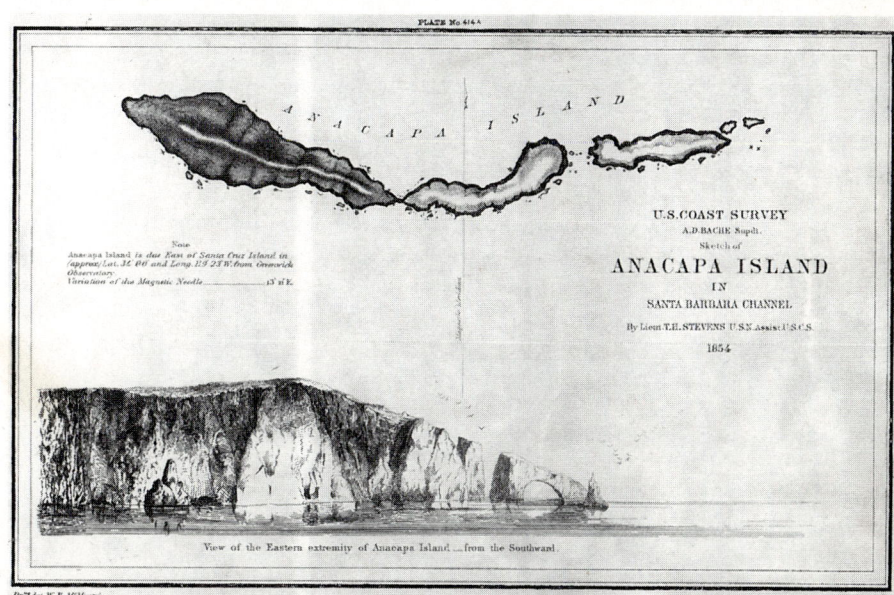

Etching of "Coast Survey No.2 Anacapa Island" by James Abbot McNeill Whistler.

Courtesy of the U. S. Coast Geodetic Survey

PROFESSIONAL SURVEYOR • January/February 1996 — 53

His supervisor, Captain Benham, who took a great interest in his friend's son, tried to induce greater regularity in his attendance by calling on him to pick him up on his way to work, but soon gave up the effort.

Whistler had rented a furnished room in a lodging house at the corner of E and 12th Streets, and through Edward de Stoeckl, the Russian minister to the United States who had been one of his father's close friends, he was enabled to enjoy the best of Washington society. As Whistler reported about his social life, "I was apt to be late, I was so busy socially . . . it was amazing how I was asked and went every where -- to balls, to the Legations, to all that was going on . . . and, when I had not a dress suit pinning up the tails of my black frock-coat, and turning it into a dress-coat for the occasion."

Despite the tedium of the work, Whistler later admitted that he had gained valuable technical instruction in the drawing and etching of government topographical maps and charts, which had to be made with the utmost accuracy and sharpness of line. His training in the art of etching was the most rigorous, and he profited considerably from it. In fact, it later became one of his specialties as an artist. The work was dull, altogether mechanical, and he sometimes relieved his boredom by filling in empty spaces on the plates with sketches of his own.

Whistler was repeatedly admonished that he was not there to spoil government plates, and again and again all his additions were ordered to be immediately erased. The plates "Coast Survey No. 1" and Coast Survey No. 2 Anacapa Island" that he produced at this time reflect his mastery of the mechanics of etching that later distinguished his career. Some of the open spaces of the first plate he filled with little sketches of people. In the latter he was responsible for the view of the eastern extremity of the island, and for the two flights of birds. These are the only two plates known to have survived from this period.

Tiny Devil in the Glass

Captain Benham periodically checked the work of each draftsmen in his department by coming to their desks and examining their work through the small magnifying glass found on each draftsman's desk. One day Whistler etched a tiny devil on his glass, and when Captain Benham used it during his inspection, he gave quite a start. He said nothing, however, but pocketed the glass and there was no further mention of the incident. Many years later an elderly gentleman appeared in Whistler's studio in Paris. Whistler failed to recognize the visitor until the now-aged Benham introduced himself by presenting the self-same magnifier.

Whistler became increasingly bored with his work, often remaining away from his desk for the entire day. He preferred not to resign but kept hoping he would be dismissed. He obtained his wish at last, after having incorporated two sea gulls, beautifully etched, upon a chart of Nantucket Sound. He left the Coast Survey in February 1855 after less than a year.

Then, resisting his brother's renewed efforts to entice him to join the locomotive works in Baltimore, Whistler obtained his mother's approval with an annual allowance of $350, and left for Paris to study art, never to return to the United States. He had read all the popular works about Bohemian life in the Latin Quarter of Paris, and to his surprise he found them to be true, and joined it gladly. Thereafter he spent the remainder of his life frequently traveling throughout Europe and oscillating between Paris and London, where he died in 1903. In the course of his career he received many honors from French, German and Italian art organizations. ∎

SILVIO BEDINI *is a historian emeritus with the Smithsonian Institution in Washington, D.C.*

ADVERTISERS INDEX

Circle	Company	Page Number	Circle	Company	Page Number
84	Accqpoint	Page 19	37	Magellan	Page 33
	ACSM Convention	Page 47	56	Mutual Industries	Page 39
114	AGA Computer	Page 46	146	NSPS/ACSM	Page 46
41	AGT	Page 43	32	Nikon	Page 14
83	Allen Precision	Pages 40 & 41	82	Pacific Crest	Page 46
34	Ashtech	Page 13	80	RAMSS	Page 15
68	Ashtech	Page 38	70	Rentec	Page 45
164	Berntsen	Page 10	63	Sarasota Computer	Page 45
29	C&G Software	Page 35	69	Schonstedt	Inside Front Cover
81	Carl Zeiss	Page 32	125	Silver Shield	Page 11
85	Chicago Steel Tape	Page 12	79	Simplicity Systems	Page 51
10	Chicago Steel Tape	Page 31	31	Soft-Art	Page 9
22	Chicago Steel Tape	Page 37	57	Sokkia	Page 5
13	DataLync Ltd.	Page 44	45	STK	Page 18
67	Geotronics	Pages 20 & 21	71	Topcon	Page 23
25	Geotronics	Inside Back Cover	72	Traverse PC	Page 16
77	Leica	Page 24 to 29	26	Trimble	Back Cover
18	Lenker	Page 46	78	Zaenkert Surveying	Page 45

LIONEL
A Collector's Guide and History

Volume V: The Archives

Other Books and Videos by Tom McComas and James Tuohy

Volumes in the Lionel Collector's Guide Series

Volume I: Prewar O Gauge
Volume II: Postwar
Volume III: Standard Gauge
Volume IV: 1970–1980
Volume V: The Archives
Volume VI: Advertising & Art

Lionel Price & Rarity Guides

Postwar 1945–1969, No. 1
Postwar 1945–1969, No. 2
Prewar 1900–1945
1970–1989
1970–1992

Books

Great Toy Train Layouts of America
Collecting Toy Trains

Videos

Lionel: The Movie
Great Layouts of America Series, Parts 1–6
Toy Train Revue Video Quarterly
The History of Lionel Trains
The Making of the Scale Hudson
Fun and Thrills with American Flyer
I Love Toy Trains
The New Lionel Showroom Layout
How to Build a Layout
Lionel Postwar
1991 Lionel Video Catalog
1992 Lionel Video Catalog

LIONEL

A Collector's Guide and History

Volume V: The Archives

Tom McComas & James Tuohy

Chilton Book Company
Radnor, Pennsylvania

Copyright © 1981 by Thomas W. McComas and James Tuohy
All Rights Reserved
Originally published in 1981 by TM Productions
Published in 1993 by Chilton Book Company

No part of this book may be reproduced, transmitted or stored in any form or by any means, electronic or mechanical, without prior written permission from the publisher

Lionel is the registered trademark of Lionel Trains, Inc., Chesterfield, Michigan. This book is neither authorized nor approved by Lionel Trains, Inc.

Library of Congress Catalog Card Number: 75-189-999
ISBN 0-8019-8511-0
Manufactured in the United States of America

In Memory of Earl Rath and Bill Ridlon

CONTENTS

Introduction	xi
History	1
Archives	7
Lift Bridge	8
The Hiawatha	10
FM Prototypes	13
Hudson Display	15
GG-1 Prototypes	16
TV Camera Car	19
6464 Prototypes	20
Alaska	26
Boys & Girls	28
Armored Train	31
Early O Gauge Set	32
K-4 Pacific	34
Waving Engineer	35
Models	36
Model Maker	37
Late Prewar Freights	38
Standard Gauge	41
Handcars	46
Wood Buildings	48
Crane & Cars	51
Diesels	52
Autos & Trucks	58
Steam Engines	62
Display Engines	65
Track	66
Timer	67
Accessories	68
Toy Show Mock-Ups	70
Ideas from Mount Clemens	72
Ideas from Irvington	74
More GG-1s & Other Electrics	77
More Standard Gauge	82
2⅞-Inch Gauge	86
Rolling Stock Prototypes	88
Rolling Stock Color Variations	93
Passenger Cars	99
Sketches & Drawings	101

INTRODUCTION

We've called this book *The Archives* even though not all the things in it are from the Lionel Archives. However, most of them were there once, and those that were not are of enough rarity or interest to have been. The Lionel archives, as has been explained in our previous books, have undergone various stages of disorganization through the years and certain things that should be there now are not.

The Fundimensions management at Mount Clemens has made great improvements in the organization of the archives, including the way things are inventoried, displayed and secured. We are grateful for the splendid cooperation of all the people at Lionel, most prominently Dan Cooney, Tom Valmassei, Bill Diss, John Brady, Denise Cassidy and Flo Lawson (who magically produced a camera for us when one of ours broke).

Many people gave us information for this book and we thank them all, but we would give special thanks to Howard Godel, the erudite author and collector, who provided knowledge and trains as well as bed, board and transportation; John DiGirolamo, the wise Johnny D, who was generous with his time and recollections; Rich Sherry, former president of the Midwest Division of the TCA, who shared his observations on prewar O gauge; Dick Branstner, whose insights are always unique; and John Palm and Dave Garrigues, whose overall advice has guided us through all our books.

Thanks also to Nancy Adams of the Chicago *Tribune;* Ed Arrigoni of the New York Bus Service; Rebecca Coleman of the London *Times;* Paula Dore of the Old Colony Train Society; Roland Hemond of the Chicago White Sox; David Allen Jones of the Chicago *Reader;* Thomas J. Shanahan of the Georgetown Reunion Association; and William L. Littlejohn, lawyer, sportsman and patron of the arts.

The book obviously would not have been possible without the cooperation of the collectors whose trains appear on these pages: Richard Cowan, Joe D'Angelo, Harry Degano, Howard Godel, James Sattler, LaRue Shempp, Joseph Siachitano, Dr. Paul Wasserman, and Cecil Yother. They were all great to us. The excellent pictures were taken by, among others: Peter Bennett (Degano's collection), Andrew Partos (Yother's), David Cornwell (Sattler's), Russ Buckingham (Godel's and Siachitano's), Ted Davis (Shempp's) and Bruce Johnson.

Finally, the authors would like to make a clarification. We take full responsibility for every word that has been published in the Lionel Series. The material is the result of interviews and conversations with hundreds of people across the country, as well as extensive research from libraries and newspaper morgues. For one of the books, Volume III, we employed a researcher, Ron Hollander, to do several interviews in the New York area. Apparently some minor confusion arose over whether he did any writing of that book or merely did research. He did no writing and should not be blamed for it. We wrote and edited the entire Volume III, as well as did the preponderance of the research. Hollander's contribution was only that of a legman, and he only worked on that one book. All the words in all our books, and all the responsibility, are ours alone.

HISTORY

The things that the Lionel Corporation made were called toy trains but the people who designed them did not really consider them toys. There was too much complicated engineering involved for that.

"Lionel was not like any other toy business," said John DiGirolamo, who was Lionel's assistant chief engineer from 1948 to 1960. "The product was very sophisticated. It took tremendous planning and design."

Therefore prototypes, the first working models, were given much attention. They were made by hand and they were inspected and modified, examined and refined until they were nearly perfect — or at least until everyone involved was satisfied that an item would work and would sell.

"In the end what we would have would be a prototype that would have everything on it we could think of — all the parts and decorations and whatever," said DiGirolamo. "If they all worked we would have a good product the first time off the assembly line, which was the purpose of paying so much attention to the prototype."

DiGirolamo, now president of Jerome Industries of Kenilworth, New Jersey, was with Lionel from 1943 until 1964, a period that included years of great success and subsequent decline. In those days (as well as in earlier years) ideas for new products would come mainly from within the company, perhaps as a result of executive meetings.

"Sometimes the choice would be made because of some hot item the railroads were advertising. If it was getting a lot of publicity — say like the 20th Century Limited — we might make it," said DiGirolamo.

Unsolicited ideas occasionally caught on, too, where someone from outside the company approached Lionel with a suggestion.

After it was agreed to make an item — the GG-1 perhaps — the road to a final prototype model split in two. One fork led to the internal design and the other to the external.

The making of the external, or "appearance model," as it was called, was handled by preliminary model builders, who, working from drawings supplied by the railroad, would make a plastic, wood or plaster model, perhaps to 1/100th scale. The model, according to DiGirolamo, was made with a certain license, with some things from the real engine eliminated or altered.

In the meantime the electrical engineers and testers were working on the motor design, the gears and other parts, trying to figure out what tools would have to be made new and what parts could be used that already existed. From all of this preliminary tinkering came new cost figures which the engineering department gave to the sales department. If projected costs were acceptable, an approval was given to proceed to the next step of prototype manufacturing.

That next step included a series of drawings, the first of which were of the parts. Each part would be drawn in detail and then in another drawing each part would be shown where it would fit into the whole. There would also be drawings of any innovative parts, those that Lionel had never made before.

Eventually all these detailed drawings would be incorporated into a large drawing, called the layout, and this would go to the model makers. These model makers were not the same ones who made the preliminary model. There were, during Lionel's peak production years, two preliminary model makers, named Lerner and Bertucci, and eight machinists who were called simply model makers.

The model makers, working from a hunk of steel or plastic or brass, would assemble the parts needed according to the drawings. Although the drawings at that point were unquestionably complex and highly detailed, they were not necessarily complete, because the model makers worked with the designers and if anything was missing they could talk it over together and decide what should be built. Key links in this process were Joe Bonanno, the chief engineer, Morris Zion, the assistant design engineer, and Gustave Ferri, a mechanic with an artist's eye.

A model was finally completed, with everything that the designers and engineers could think was needed, including the decoration and internal workings. That model was called the prototype, but the tinkering still had not stopped.

A final presentation was made to the sales department and usually there were a few suggestions made and the prototype was modified a little bit more. Ultimately there was a final approval given and then a set of final engineering drawings was made. These were to be used by outside manufacturers who might be contracted to make parts. These drawings were also reviewed several times before they were approved.

Actually, in the days following World War II and going through the 50s, Lionel had extensive manufacturing capabilities of its own and most of their parts were made within the company, although, of course, the final engineering drawing still had to be made.

"We utilized the facilities of the plant as much as possible, said DiGirolamo." We had a tremendous toolmaking department, good for making die-casting molds, plastic molds and assembling parts.

"Lionel really was a first class manufacturing company. At that time we were the leaders in die-casting, powder, metalurgy, and plastic finishing.

Ironically, Lionel's very proficiency in production and leadership in technology worked against it. Often, it would have been more economical to have outside manufacturers make parts — as Lionel currently does — than keep the large facilities and many employees it took to maintain their own manufacturing capabilities. Eventually, the extensive overhead contributed to Lionel losses of the late 1950s.

"It was a major problem," said DiGirolamo. "It was a big burden, but there were a couple of reasons why we kept making our own tools. First, right after the war everybody was rebuilding, there were shortages of everything and it wasn't easy to get things done. Second, we were pioneers in so many things, there was no one else who could do them. Later on, though, we probably should have been using outside vendors faster than we did."

After the various production control decisions were arrived at, the tools were made and production started. The prototype's time was over. It had been studied, copied and shown at the toy fair and it now probably rested on a shelf. If, at the toy fair, the prototype had failed to capture interest, mass production plans were cancelled, but in the growth days of the post-war years that did not often happen. As one former Lionel salesman said, "You could do no wrong. You went there and you just wrote orders."

While the toy fair orders would probably not result in the cancellation of an item, they did influence the type of tools that would be made for it. If orders totalled 10,000 units, one type of tool would be made, but if orders totalled 50,000 units, which would result in a two or three year run, a more substantial tool would be made.

Even after the toy fair and the beginning of production, the refinement on the final product did not end.

"There were always a lot of ideas that came out when production started," said DiGirolamo. "Ideas about assembly, about what other parts might go into the piece, once the production people saw the prototype. Some were good ideas, some bad ideas. There was always a little confusion in the production. Every once in a while someone would come up with a new tool that could make something cheaper. Many people were sort of fighting to find a mistake so they could come up with a way to correct it. It was good. That was the way Mario Caruso, who ran the factory, wanted it. The employee competition resulted in a better product."

Mario Caruso, it turned out, was the Supreme Commander of the Lionel factory, exercising an influence that not even Joshua Lionel Cowen intruded upon. Cowen, although a frequent visitor to the factory, left its running to Caruso, an Italian immigrant who started with the company in 1910 and rose to be secretary-treasurer and a major stockholder. His family were tool makers in Italy and Caruso, besides his Lionel duties, was much involved in a family factory, named LaPrecisa, in the old country. Caruso's influence at Lionel, as well as his interests back in Italy, may explain why the dies for the great 700EW Hudson were made there.

Caruso, according to reports, created a system of management that depended on bitter competition among executives who battled each other for new ideas.

"There was tremendous infighting, unbelievable rivalries," said DiGirolamo, who began his career at the end of Caruso's era. "The only way up the management ladder was to have an idea for some new product or process. One of the biggest rivalries was among Joe Bonanno, the chief engineer, Charles Giaimo the production manager, and Mario Caruso. Everybody was trying to better the other guy's ideas — trying to get to the top. One guy trying to beat the other guy out. It worked very well. Everybody worked hard. One of the biggest cases of infighting developed over the smoke pellet. Everybody wanted credit for it because they knew it was going to be a big item. Even after Caruso left in 1945 there was tremendous rivalry. One big fight was over who developed the whistle. Cowen gave credit to Giaimo, who was Caruso's brother-in-law (there were many Caruso relatives at Lionel, including his nephew and later Personnel Director Philip Marfuggi). That made Joe Bonnano mad."

Caruso disliked, according to DiGirolamo, any ostentatious living on the part of his executives. "Nobody drove a car more expensive than a Ford, including Mario, and he didn't want them buying summer homes on the sea shore. He believed in a certain immigrant ethic, that the bosses should never get too far removed from the workers."

Caruso treated the workers on the line with a kind of stern respect, implying that they could drive themselves harder than they knew. He received maximum effort for less than maximum pay.

"But he ruled with an iron hand," said DiGirolamo. "When he walked through the factory everyone would shake. He was a small dynamic type who was hard-driving but you couldn't tell his emotions. He was a one-man band. During the war, Larry Cowen got involved in the company and tried to run the plant. That didn't sit well with Mario Caruso and finally, in a last power struggle, he left."

Caruso had invented a cigarette vending machine and when he left Lionel in 1945 he started to manufacture the machines in Staten Island. He did quite well at it and eventually sold out to Seeburg. Mario Caruso, now in his 90s, lives in retirement in a large villa in Italy.

Cigarette vending machines were developed by Caruso for Lionel around 1945, when the company had begun to think in terms of diversification. They had developed several products which would have been successful sellers, but cash considerations prevented them from putting them on the market. In addition to vending machines, Lionel had developed a motorized bicycle, an outboard motor, and they were first with a room air-conditioner. They were also considering a line of wooden toys.

All those things would require considerable investments and before the war, the company did not have it. During the war they were involved in war production. After the war it took time to accumulate the money, and Cowen was also slowing down. Finally, one by one, other companies came on the market with products which Lionel had developed first.

"While they had the ideas and prototypes, they couldn't organize the manufacture at that time, said DiGirolamo. Think of putting two or three million dollars into those projects. Lionel wasn't ready. A few more years and they would have been, but then it was too late."

There were several things Lionel got into too late, such as slot cars and HO and, in DiGirolamo's opinion, there was at least one thing they should not have gotten into at all.

"In the 1930s, what the public wanted was HO, but without much investigation Lionel spent $100,000 on OO. But only the train hobbyists wanted OO, not the public. So it was not successful."

DiGirolamo admits to partial responsibility for Lionel's failure to participate in the early slot cars trend. He was told by Joe Bonanno to study the slot car market.

"I made my report and said that slot cars were a departure from the standard idea of Lionel. I said they wouldn't go any place."

DiGirolamo started his career at Lionel during World War II when he saw an ad in the paper that they needed an engineer. Just a few weeks out of college, he answered the ad and got the job.

"But I was there three days before I knew they made trains," he said. "All I saw around were compasses and other equipment they were making for the Navy. In fact, when I was being interviewed for the job by Bonanno, I wondered why there was a train on the shelf behind him."

He soon learned, and after the war he designed several items and received seven patents, including the 1033 transformer.

"It was a good place to work back then," he said. "It was really, in management, a bunch of young people growing up together just after the war. I was 29 when I was made head of the electrical engineering department. Rex Marfuggi was head of production when he was 32. The opportunity was there."

One person who never was an employee of Lionel but who did some work for them once was Raymond Loewy, the famous industrial designer. Counting on the Loewy name to help sales, Cowen commissioned him to design a coal loader, which was later manufactured.

"The only thing was, it took Loewy or one of his students a month to come up with a design," said DiGirolamo. "It was just one picture, one rendition, and he charged $6,000 for it.

"There was another designer we used to work with named Peter Van Dyke, who we had on a retainer one or two days a week. We would sit down with him and think of ideas and he would produce five or six drawings in one day and charge $300 for it."

Making a drawing or having an idea was only the first part of the solution, of course. The idea had to be made to work and that was a job that often fell to Frank Pettit, a man of considerable engineering skills (see Volume III) who was responsible for many Lionel patents. Pettit, who married Mario Caruso's niece, had a little room all to himself which functioned as his own preliminary model shop and he would study the drawings made by designers and try to figure out a way to make them work. That he was successful is attested to by the fact that his name is on the patents for many pieces, including the merchandise car, the barrel and log unloading cars, the remote control electric coupler, and the newspaper vendor with dog.

One item that did not come out of product development at Lionel was the operating milk car, which was brought in by a young man, partially handicapped, who had the foresight to be accompanied by a lawyer. Lionel liked the automatic milk car — one of the most popular items it ever made — and the young man was one of the few outsiders who ever received royalties from Lionel, and he received a lot of them.

Many Lionel prototypes and special items are now in the hands of private collectors. The question often arises how these invaluable items ever got out of the factory. One answer is, of course, that these items were not always invaluable, or at least no one thought they were. What are now valuable paint samples — sets or cars that were made in unique colors for test purposes — or one-of-a-kind color variations often left the factory in the simplest of manners. They were given away.

"Lionel was very particular about quality control of their colors," said Mrs. Teresa Natolli, who worked at Lionel from 1926 until 1946. "Anything that had a variation in color was put into a large bin. At Christmas time employees could take out the sets or cars they wanted and take them home to their children."

Some prototypes were stolen through the years, but many of those were given away, too. Louis Napoliello, who once had more postwar prototypes than any other collector in the United States, got them from his friend Pat Papa, who was production manager in 1969 when the New Jersey factory closed down.

"Here," Papa said to Napoliello one day, pointing to a closet in the engineering department that was full of prototypes. "Take them."

They don't do things like that at Lionel any more.

Mario Caruso

Joshua Lionel Cowen

Arthur Raphael

Charles V. Giaimo

Joseph I. Bonanno

Philip H. Marfuggi

Lawrence Cowen

John DiGirolamo

ARCHIVES

The Lionel archives were in a state of flux for a long time because of the folding of the factory in New Jersey, the eventual move to Mount Clemens and several moves and switches of management in Michigan. The archives have even been moved since the authors last wrote about them in Volume IV. At that time, in the summer of 1979, the archives were tucked away in an upstairs room of the Lionel factory. They were in a state of semi-disarray, although an extensive job of reorganization was already underway, led by Project Engineer Bill Diss. Now, in the summer of 1981, the archives are located on the second floor of the headquarters and administration building of Fundimensions.

All the old regular production items have been placed on shelves in numerical order according to type. Prototypes are kept together on different shelves. The room is locked at all times and only a small number of people have access to it.

Those pre-1970 things that could not be fitted into the new room have been packed away in boxes and stored in another room in the headquarters building. The room in the factory that was cleared out by the transfer of the archives will still be used. Fundimension prototypes will be stored there as they are created, but the majority of the space will be used to store samples of production items. The policy is to put what are called "master cartons" of production items in the room. A master carton is a packing unit which contains three to six samples of a production piece. The master carton for the Norfolk and Western steamer, for example, contained three engines and three tenders. These were the first three engines and tenders off the assembly line.

Not all the future Fundimensions prototypes will be saved, only those of the better items. The more common, end-of-the-line things will either be destroyed or repainted and used again. Even with the prototypes of the better stuff, however, there is a chance some will not be saved.

"They go to shows all over the country," said Diss. "They are sent to various photography studios. They are constantly being packed and repacked. Some just don't survive the handling. If they do, though, and we have no further use for them, we will put them in the archives."

The idea of creating a Lionel museum is still active, especially in the mind of John Brady, Lionel's able public relations man. He would like to see a room, separate from the archives, where prototypes and other interesting items would be on public display.

When Fundimensions secured the rights to the Lionel name they also obtained the American Flyer name and what was left of American Flyer archives. It consisted of less than 50 prototypes, a small inventory of parts and perhaps 300 production pieces, both O and S gauges.

"The most important thing we got from Flyer," said Diss, "was all the records telling us about tools — all the process sheets, material specs, plus a lot of the drawings and blueprints of individual parts."

The Flyer archives are packed in boxes and will be kept in the room in the factory along with the future Fundimensions prototypes.

LIFT BRIDGE

Lionel Archives

Private Collection

These pictures show the prototype and an earlier working model of the 213 Lift Bridge. The prototype was used in a picture for the 1950 catalog but the bridge was never put into production. The earlier model, as can be seen, was much more primitive, although both bridges worked the same way. It was the workings, as a matter of fact, that led to the decision not to make the 213. The design was extremely complicated and was not practical for mass production.

THE HIAWATHA

Lionel Archives

The Hiawatha is one of the great O-gauge collector's prizes of the prewar era. Actually, the colorful Hiawatha is a proud trophy for collectors of any era. The prototype had a strange little design on the nose emblem where on the real engine was the train number. On the production model a Lionel L replaced the scratchy design, which most resembles an Indian sign.

Collectors might one day see a return of the cherished prewar items, like the Hiawatha, in both Standard and O gauge. It would, according to the people at Mount Clemens, all depend on demand.

"We could easily do it," said Bill Diss, who as project engineer is the man in the best position to know. "There is nothing to prevent us from making all the good items, like the State Set and Hiawatha. Some of the tin-stamp tooling is missing but we have all of the die-cast tooling. The tin-stamp tooling is not that expensive. Detail was added to those prewar items with little stampings and we do a lot of stampings now. E units, side rods and motor plates are all stampings.

"If we thought there was a market we would go into it. The way we find out if there is a market is to take a market survey and we'll probably do that in the next two years. If management thinks the market is there, we will make them. We won't go into prewar stamped trains because we are out of ideas in plastic — I don't see us exhausting postwar O gauge — we will get into it as an additional source of business."

Private Collection

The 027 gauge Hiawatha prototype. No tender or cars have ever been located. The prototype used the motor and side rods from the 1684 steamer. The pilot and trailing trucks apparently were also from the 1684.

LaRue Shempp Collection

LaRue Shempp Collection

James M. Sattler Collection

FM PROTOTYPES

The Lackawanna, Southern Pacific and Reading FM Train Master prototypes were shown at the New York and Anaheim toy fairs in 1954 but only the Lackawanna was produced. Western orders did not justify production of the Southern Pacific and skimpy Eastern orders eliminated the Reading. The Lackawanna, when it came off the production line, was changed somewhat. The colors of the roof and lettering were different and so were the roof screens and the pilot. The graphics on the production model were less colorful, the yellow stripe on the ends being eliminated. The Jersey Central prototype of 1956, which resembled the Reading, also differed from the production model. Perhaps they shouldn't have changed it because the orange and blue production model, numbered 2341, never did sell well.

James M. Sattler Collection

LaRue Shempp Collection

Besides the prototype Southern Pacific, Lionel made several other pre-production SPs, which they gave to executives of the railroad in 1954. These models differed from the prototype in several ways, as can be seen by looking at the model above, which is in the collection of LaRue Shempp.

When, in the fall of 1978 Fundimensions decided to bring out the Southern Pacific FM, they choose to make it like the Shempp version. However, although they had drawings made, they still did not have a model to show in January of 1979, as the toy fairs approached. They borrowed one from TM Productions, which previously had one made up, using drawings provided by Lionel, for a 1979 calendar photograph. The TM model had not been intended to be a prototype but it became one when Lionel Public Relations manager John Brady took it to the New York, Chicago and San Francisco shows and then had it photographed for the 1979 Lionel catalog.

The Lionel production model of the Southern Pacific turned out to be a little more detailed than the TM prototype photographed for the catalog. The red and gray warning stripes replaced the single red stripe which ran on the bottom of the front and rear ends of the prototype. Fundimensions has not skimped on decorations, as is explained in the **GG-1** section on page 17. The blue on the original postwar **2331** Virginian FM, for instance, came from an unpainted blue plastic shell, while the gray shell of the 8950 Virginian by Fundimensions was painted a rich and glossy blue, a more expensive procedure.

Author's Collection

HUDSON DISPLAY

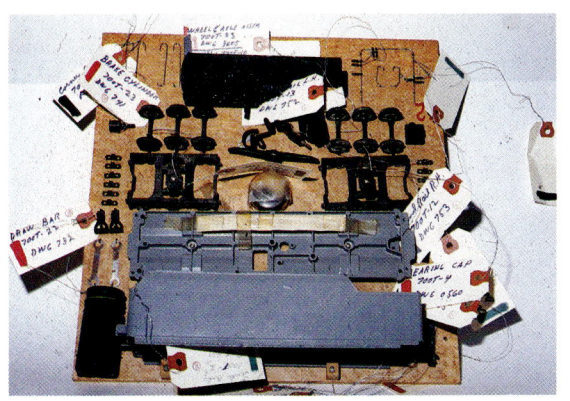 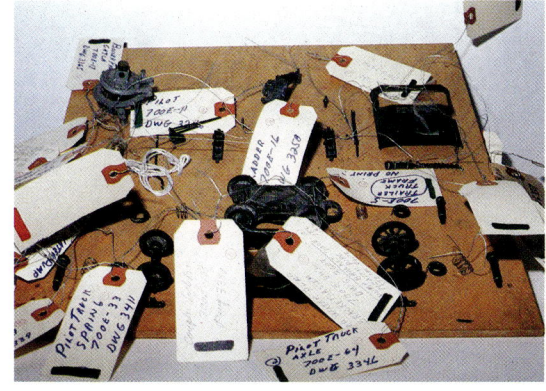

Lionel Archives

Lionel made a display board, holding each part that went into the engine, to promote their new scale Hudson kit in 1938. The tags shown in the pictures were added years later by the engineers at Fundimensions. At left a picture from a dealer display catalog showing the six boards with Hudson parts.

GG-1 PROTOTYPES

Gerald Raup Collection

Lionel Archives

First Fundamensions prototype experimenting with glossy paint.

These are prototype models for the GG-1 from both 1947 and 1981. When Lionel announced the original GG-1 in the 1947 catalog, the picture was of an engine with the number 4911, an actual Pennsylvania Railroad number. But when the production model came off the assembly line, the number was 2332, strictly Lionel. As can be seen, the Lionel prototype was made with the 4911 number on it, indicating some thought was given to using a prototypical number, as Lionel had with the Hudson numberboards.

There were several other differences between that original prototype and the 1947 production model: the hand-made model had a brass body and chassis and the trucks and side frames had brass parts; the green was darker than the production model; the insulators were procelain and secured by screws; all the trim was decaled instead of heat-stamped; there were grab-irons on the doorways, nose, and pilot trucks; celluloid was placed behind the windows; the nose was more rounded on the prototype.

Lionel Archives　　　　　　　　　　　　　　　Early and late prototypes, showing changes in striping.

Fundimensions made its first GG-1 in 1977, the Tuscan 8753 and followed the next year with the black Penn Central, 8850. In 1981 Fundimensions introduced its first Brunswick green GG-1, and several mechanical changes were made: a problem with oil dripping on the tracks was corrected by shortening the motor shaft; new flat wheels on the pilot replaced tapered wheels that wobbled; and the magnets for Magne-Traction were staked on rather than glued (see Volume IV, pages 77 and 109 for more detail on the problems with the old GG-1s).

There were also cosmetic changes, and how these came about are shown in the pictures. Lionel's Project Engineer, Bill Diss, first experimented with a glossy green paint and a prototype was made to see how it looked. This model had stripes similar to the 8753 Tuscan GG-1 and had a Lionel number of 8052. The glossy paint was approved and next, said Diss, "We decided to use the prototypical number of 4935 and to make the lettering smaller and more extended. The idea was to give the illusion of length." A second prototype was made incorporating those changes. In a third change, Diss narrowed the five stripes and ran them above the ladders, eliminating the break in the lines present in all previous GG-1s, postwar and Fundimensions. "Our new GG-1 looks about three inches longer than the old one," said Diss. Bill Diss did not know it as he searched for a way to make the GG-1 look more realistic, but the changes he made brought the Lionel GG-1 full circle. The 1981 model was decorated almost exactly like the 1947 prototype. Note the small, elongated typefaces on each, the placing of all five stripes above the ladders, and the use of a Pennsylvania prototypical number. In 1981, for the first time in 34 years, the GG-1 was made the way it had been originally conceived.

The green GG-1, when it appeared in 1981, was met with praise from collectors. One called it the finest piece Lionel ever made, in any era. Other comments sampled by the authors were nearly as complimentary, although one collector said he thought the color was a little too light. The near unanimity of good opinion was reached in spite of the GG-1's glossy finish.

The glossy versus flat finish has been the subject of dispute both in and out of Lionel. Some collectors did not like the glossy finish on the Southern Crescent and Blue Comet engines, for instance, and complained about it to Lionel. Some executives at Lionel don't like the glossy finish either. The collectors don't like it because it is foreign looking to them — old Lionel did not use it on their engines. The

Lionel Archives

Second Fundimensions prototype with new number but old markings.

people within Lionel who are against it are usually as motivated by the fact that it cost more to paint an engine glossy — and presents other manufacturing difficulties — as they are by aesthetic considerations.

The way Lionel puts on a gloss is to first paint the engine flat and then add a clear coat of laquer-like paint. To do it flat would be cheaper. In addition, after painting, if an item is chipped on the assembly line, it has to be painted with the flat again and then the glossy. Glossy paint itself is harder to work with than flat, especially lead-free paint which, starting in 1981, Lionel was required to use by law.

"Lead-free paint doesn't cover as well," said Bill Diss, Project Engineer at Lionel, and one of the advocates of gloss paint. "But you can't overload it because if you do it turns to a milky color. So you want to spray it wet, but that leads to dripping problems. The manufacturing department doesn't like using it."

Another reason manufacturing looks with disfavor at glossy paint is that it doesn't hide imperfections in castings as well as flat paint. That means more sanding and smoothing.

Diss defended the use of glossy paint, however. He claimed that it was more realistic to have a glossy finish on a new engine.

"Hardly anybody ever saw the old steamers and diesels when they were first off the assembly line, but they were glossy too," he said. "We have a picture of a new GG-1 from the 1930s and it was just as glossy as Lionel's. I like to make things as prototypical as possible, but we cannot always do that. Price considerations for making a new die may prevent a certain Lionel model from looking exactly like its prototype. An example of that is the tender for the Norfolk that should be larger but isn't. There are certain things we cannot do in the manufacturing process, but as far as I'm concerned paint is not one of them. If it was glossy on the prototype, it should be glossy on the model."

So, in spite of the expense and the fact that quality control at Lionel will reject more engines with glossy paint than they will with flat, Diss and some others fight for accuracy. The 1981 GG-1 would seem to justify the fight.

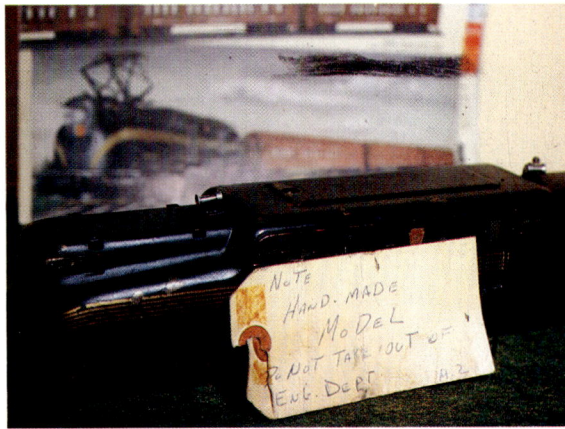

Gerald Raup Collection

TV CAMERA CAR

An operating TV Camera Car prototype. The car, never produced, would have been activated by remote control track, the way operating boxcars were activated. It was reset by hand.

Lionel Archives

6464 PROTOTYPES

The 6464 cars, as they say, are ever popular. When they were first introduced in 1953, they were longer and higher than the earlier O gauge boxcars, the colors were brighter and the graphics were splashier. They were immediately popular and they still are. There were 29 different number designations and so many variations, from the immediately obvious to the persistently obscure, that no one seems to know them all.

Essentially, the 6464 car is still being made by General Mills, in the 9200-9700-9400 series. The graphics are a little better on the new cars and so are the paint jobs. The main change has not been on the bodies but on the wheels, which are now tapered with fixed, live axles.

The following pages contain some prototype 6464s that were considered but never came about, as well as a few of the off-beat that came off the production line but not in any significant numbers.

Great Northern 6464 prototype, postwar era. Never produced.

This Kansas, Oklahoma & Gulf prototype was never produced. In a way it was too bad. Short lines have a certain rustic charm to them.

Lionel Archives

It is unusual for a "built date" to appear on a prototype, which means that this Detroit and Mackinac 6464 car came very close to going into production in 8/58.

Lionel Archives

The prototype of a 6464 boxcar planned for 1959 but never produced. It was made eventually by Fundimensions — three times — but never exactly the way the original prototype was made.

Harry Degano Collection

The 6464-1 Western Pacific in orange rather than silver. The silver Western Pacific was the first 6464 car produced. The second was the orange Great Northern. This car was supposed to have the Great Northern marking, but the new shell got stamped with Western Pacific before the Great Northern stamps were put on the marking machines.

Harry Degano Collection

The 6464-25 Great Northern came in orange, not Tuscan. However, the orange Great Northern was the second 6464 car made by Lionel and was followed in the line by the 6464-50 Minneapolis and St. Louis in Tuscan. A few Tuscan bodies were stamped with the Great Northern markings before the stamps were changed to Minneapolis and St. Louis.

James M. Sattler Collection

This 6464-125 Pacemaker came in unusual lilac with bright red letters and no top stripe.

Lionel Archives

This Burlington 6464 prototype was never produced in the postwar era. It is almost identical to the 9436 Burlington made in 1981 by Fundimensions. It came in the Great Lakes set.

23

Lionel Archives

This 6464 boxcar shell was sitting on a shelf in the archives. It had 6464-900 NYC decals on a gold body, instead of the usual jade green body. Somebody was toying around with an idea, apparently, but no one can say for sure what it was. That is one of the fascinating things about probing the archives. Little mysteries.

Lionel Archives

This U.S. Air Force 6464 prototype was never produced.

James M. Sattler Collection

The regular production 6464-525 Minneapolis and St. Louis was red, this one, probably a color sample, is bright pink-purple.

24

This 6464-900 New York Central boxcar has no red lettering or black trim around the NYC box. It is not known for sure whether this was a prototype, a color sample model or was just a factory error.

James M. Sattler Collection

Private Collection

Seaboard 6464 boxcar prototype, never produced.

Private Collection

Prototype 6464-500 Timken. Markings are decaled.

ALASKA

Harry Degano Collection

James M. Sattler Collection

The 6464-825 Alaska boxcar is very hard to find in good condition. The production model was blue painted over a gray plastic body. The slightest chip on the body made the gray show through the blue. The lettering was yellow. Shown on this page are three variations, probably paint samples, of an already hard-to-find car. One has white letters, numbers, stripe and door (which was blue on production model); a second has white letters and numbers and stripe; the third has white letters and numbers and a yellow stripe.

James M. Sattler Collection

As 1959 approached, Lionel was planning an Alaska Set, in honor of the state that entered the Union that year. They had a prototype GP-9 made and then even had a number placed on another mock-up, but they finally decided to make the set lower priced and had it headed by the 614 switcher. The Alaska GP-9 was never produced.

Gaetano J. D'Angelo Collection

James M. Sattler Collection

Cecil Yother Collection

27

BOYS & GIRLS

In 1957 Lionel toyed with the idea of adding a blue Boy's Train to the line, along with the pink Girl's Train that did come out that year. But in the end Lionel's braintrust decided against full production of a Boy's Train, although a very few, perhaps as few as three or four, were made (See Volume II, page 69). Of the blue-engined Boy's Trains known to exist, all are headed by a 2018 steamer except one, which is shown here. This is the only known blue 2055 ever made. The engine had smoke and Magne-Traction and the tender had a whistle and automatic coupler. The numbering and lettering were heat-stamped on the engine and tender.

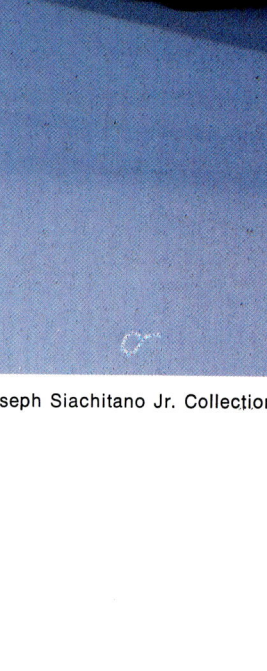

Joseph Siachitano Jr. Collection

Harry Degano Collection

The 2037 Girl's Train engine with black lettering rather than blue.

Harry Degano Collection

The 6446-25 Girl's Train hopper in pink with black lettering. The usual way the Girl's Train hopper came was lilac with purple markings.

Girl's Train caboose is usually blue with white lettering.

For "O" Gauge Track

No. 215 Armored Motor and Supply Car Outfit

BANG! It's New

Outfit No. 213: comprises one No. 203 Armored Motor Car, 7½ inches long, with eight sections of "O" gauge curved track, making a circle 28½ inches in diameter. One section has terminals for connecting to transformer or batteries.
Price complete, attractively packed - - $5.00
Code Word "LIBERTY"

Outfit No. 215: comprises one No. 203 Armored Motor Car, 7½ inches long; and two No. 702 Supply Cars, each 7½ inches long, equipped with two 4 wheel trucks and two sliding center doors, enamelled in battleship gray; also has eight sections of "O" gauge curved and two sections O.S. straight track, making an oval 39 x 28½ inches. One section of track has terminals for connecting to transformer or batteries; also includes one No. 88 controlling rheostat.
Price complete, attractively packed - - $8.00
Code Word "GLORY"

Another LIONEL TRIUMPH

No. 213. Armored Motor for "O" Gauge Track

LIONEL ARMORED MOTOR CAR AND TRAINS

Always Ahead in Ideas

Setting the pace—right in the forefront—here we again present to buyers another new and concrete idea—ready to sell—timely—at a price mighty attractive to your customers—at a profit satisfying to you!

Timely—Ringing with War Atmosphere

How the martial spirit now flames out of us—from the youngster up to grandpa! The children must imitate the grown-ups. We have met this seasonable demand by this brand new, electrically operated gun battery on tracks, with its own motive power.

True to Models

The Outfits are faithful copies on a small scale of those new and terrifying siege guns now being operated on specially built temporary tracks on the battlefields of Europe. The bodies of these monsters are formed out of heavy sheet steel. The die work brings out every detail of the heavy riveted plates, ventilators, doors, etc., and is typical of Lionel construction.

[...] detail is the battleship gray enamel in which they are finished.

[...] revolving turret upon which two long miniature guns are mounted [...] ful reproduction of the original. The motor is similar to those [...] "O" Gauge Outfits and is powerful enough to haul any [...] ail cars, which are enamelled in the same battleship gray as [...] One of these Armored trains makes a wonderful addition [...] outfit, or by the purchase of the Motor Car by itself. [...] cars, etc., can be added from time to time.

Trade Orders Show Expected Interest

[...] responding with immediate orders, as we antici[...] There will be no disappointments on delivery, for we are [...] ready for your order. Only, order at once!

Order by Return Mail

[...] catalog will reach tens of thousands of boys who [...] advertisements will stir up new and old customers for [...] send them your way.

Advertised Nationally

Remember that these Armored Trains will be seen from the [...] to the Pacific in our advertisements in all [...] papers as well as in the big national [...] See our list of National Mediums, in [...] our advertisements will appear. You need [...] told how these advertisements send the [...]

Remember: Lionel profit is GOOD profit.

THE LIONEL MFG. COMPANY
48-52 EAST 21st STREET
NEW YORK CITY

Outfit No. 214: comprises one No. 203 Armored Motor Car, as described above; two No. 900 Ammunition Cars (each 6 inches long) enamelled in battleship gray—same as armored car. Outfit includes eight sections curved track, making circle 28½ inches in diameter, one section having terminals for connecting with transformer or batteries; outfit also has one No. 88 controlling rheostat.
Price complete, attractively packed - $6.50
Code word "VICTORY"

Car Outfit No. 214. For "O" Gauge Track
Armored Motor and Ammunition

LIONEL TRAINS ARE ALWAYS REALISTIC

"Seventeen years standard of the world" has been earned by faithful adherence to this fundamental manufacturing principle formulated in 1900 by Mr. Cowen: "Always stick closely to the actual types or big models of locomotives, coaches, box cars, semaphores, etc., in making the miniatures." Why? Because, as the boy is a small edition of the man and imitates him, so he enjoys playing with models that resemble faithfully what men operate. *This cannot be truly said of any other line.* The steel construction—the electric lighting systems—the rich enameled colors—the symmetry of outline—the grace and elegance of each piece—the whole ensemble—give all Lionel Productions a surprising realism and beauty which make them SELL and STAY SOLD.

THE BOYS WILL SELL 'EM for YOU STOCK UP LIBERALLY NOW

ARMORED TRAIN

James M. Sattler Collection

The 1917 Army Train, offered in the year America entered World War I, came in three cataloged versions: the engine alone, the engine and two 900 ammunition cars, and the engine and two 702 supply cars. All versions are very rare and hardly ever found in one collection, especially in the fine shape that Jim Sattler of Honolulu has them. At left is the dealer flyer Lionel used to advertise the new train.

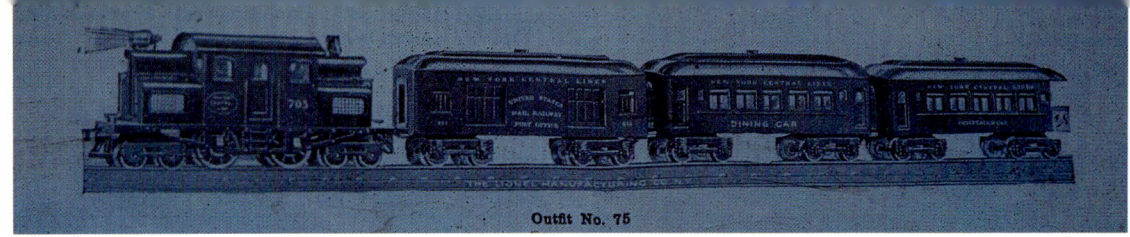

Outfit No. 75

EARLY O GAUGE SET

The 703 set shown above was probably the first O Gauge set Lionel ever made. The 703 production set was made in 1915 and the set in the photograph was an early pre-production model. The prototype differs somewhat from the artist's rendition that appeared in the 1915 catalog. The mock-up had a Pullman car "Dining Car."

The 703 engine, the production model, is itself quite rare. Only about eight are known to exist and those that do have some differences from the prototype. The wire used on the protoype was heavier than on the production model; the handrails were bent at the point they entered the frame instead of being straight; the journal boxes were brass instead of stamped; the main wheels were spoked and painted red instead of being solid; and the pony wheels were solid instead of spoked. The prototype's door screens were painted gold.

Dr. Paul Wasserman Collection

WITH BAGGAGE CAR

On all the production models known they were the same color as the body.

The passenger cars on the prototype contained a crude lighting system, although production model O Gauge passenger cars didn't have lights until 1924. The Pullman and observation cars had five windows with small lavatory windows at each end. Production models had six larger windows and no lavatory windows. The vestibule ends, outlined in black on the prototype, were not on the production models. Roofs on two of the mockup cars had simulated vents, while the other roof was flat, suggesting the thrown-together quality of many early prototypes.

The existence of a baggage car on the prototype indicates that at one time there were plans to make one. But none of the sets in existence have that 611 baggage car. The prototype stands alone. For more about the 703 set see Volume I, page 80.

K-4 PACIFIC

In 1947 Lionel brought out their version of a K-4 Pacific steamer. It was not a true Pacific, since the wheel configuration was 2-6-2 instead of 4-6-2. But, as these photographs show, Lionel once had plans for a 4-6-2. The model department produced a hand-built brass chassis and steam chest and then added the Berkshire mechanism minus a set of drivers. They then modified the 225E boiler casting and the working model was an accurate reproduction of a K-4 Pacific, but it was never made. It would have had to sell for the same price as the Berkshire and Lionel wanted a lower-priced locomotive. They compromised by eliminating the new chassis and using the same one that the 225 used, with the same 2-6-2 wheel alignment (see Volume II, page 49).

Lionel Archives

WAVING ENGINEER

The waving engineer was an interesting item Lionel developed in the late 1940s but never made. The engineer was attached to a device that ran down to the drawbar and when the drawbar moved on turns the engineer would stick his head out the window, his arm extended as if he were waving. It was a nice effect but the Lionel people decided the engineer was too small to be seen easily.

Lionel Archives

Lionel Archives

MODELS

Lionel Archives

The prototype tender for the 0-6-0 switcher is brass. The 1656 in the middle picture is a production model with a production smoke element added to it, suggesting Lionel was entertaining the idea of adding smoke to the switchers. The mock-up in the bottom picture was one of four made for the 1948 Toy Fair in San Francisco. They had prewar motors and sintered steel wheels.

LaRue Shempp Collection

Cecil Yother Collection

MODEL MAKER

Lionel Archives

This hand-made model was to be the prototype for a Walt Disney-style loco in the mid-1970s. The plan was to make an old-fashioned-type engine to go along with the General. The plan was discarded when the cost of the dies for the engine and six-wheel mechanism was too high.

This prototype was the work of Bruno Branstner, for several years Fundimensions top model maker. Bruno, shown at work in the picture on the right, looked delightfully what he was: a little old German toymaker. Branstner, whose son Richard, was the first head of engineering at the new Lionel in Mount Clemens, started his career as a dental lab technician, making teeth models. "Everything

Bruno did had a special touch to it," said Dan Johns, Lionel's service manager, and he was responsible for a lot of things. That Disney engine, for instance, compare it to other prototypes and you'll see it is almost scale and had nice detailing to it that many prototypes did not have. Look at the detailing on the walkways. Bruno was always tinkering, always had something going." Sadly, Bruno Branstner was killed in an automobile accident on his way to work one morning in 1975.

LATE PREWAR FREIGHTS

In 1940 Lionel made a number of changes on their large O gauge freight cars, the main ones being the elimination of the nickel and brass trim, which were replaced by rubber-stamped markings. New trucks were added and moved towards the ends of the cars. Paint colors were changed. Some of the early cars off the assembly line, which should have been rubber-stamped, had nickel trim. They are all extremely rare. These two pages show a few.

Richard Cowan Collection

This 2812 Terra Cotta gondola should have had rubber stamping but has nickel plates and trim. Five are known to exist.

Richard Cowan Collection

This rubber-stamped hopper is supposed to have automatic couplers, not manual ones, and be numbered 2816. Six like this are known to exist.

Richard Cowan Collection

This 816 hopper has the late trucks, trim and paint but still has nickel plates. Seven are known to exist.

Richard Cowan Collection

This caboose has the late trucks, trim and colors but has nickel plates instead of white rubber-stamping. Eight are known to exist.

Richard Cowan Collection

Richard Cowan Collection

The 813 rubber-stamped Stock Car is rare enough that one collector bought an entire collection just to get the piece. Now we discover a variation. One car has an unpainted nickel handle on the door, the other has the nickel handle painted, which is the variation.

Richard Cowan Collection

The 813 Stock Car came with either a pea green or a maroon roof and door guides. It was not reported ever appearing with an orange roof and door guides. Since this car could be easily faked by replacing the roof and door guides with those from an 814 Boxcar, we examined it very carefully. It appears to be original, based on the fact that the tabs that secure the door guides to the body have not been tampered with.

STANDARD GAUGE

A very early 418 Baggage Car with the very rare Illinois Central markings. The car commonly came with Lionel Lines or New York Central markings.

Private Collection

Now these are *really* what you would call hand-made prototypes. They are 115 tank cars. The bodies are wood, the frames a bent piece of tin, like the 11 flat car, and the spigots on top are bent nails.

Private Collection

This number 1910 loco, made in 1910, was repainted by the Lionel factory and numbered 53. Such repainting was not uncommon in those days. They just wanted to sell the stuff.

The 400E in black with a red frame stripe is probably not a prototype but it is so rare it might as well be one.

Private Collection

Private Collection

The Early Period Standard Gauge passenger cars, dating back to about 1910, consisted of an 18 Pullman, 19 Combine and 190 Observation. This is the only known dining car.

Private Collection

The "Trolley Body" 29 Day Coach was the very first passenger car Lionel offered for sale. It got its name from the fact that when Lionel first advertised a passenger car, they didn't actually have one; so in 1908 they took the body from a 3 Trolley, painted it green, stamped 29 on it, and called it their new No. 29 Day Coach. These first version day coaches were stamped NYC & HRR between the gold stripes that ran beneath the windows. This is a photograph of the only known trolley body 29 Day Coach that was marked Pennsylvania.

Private Collection

This 422 Tempel Blue Comet car was part of a unique set that had dark blue bodies and black roofs to go with a dark blue and black 400E.

Private Collection

Lionel was messing around with colors again. This is the Tempel Blue Comet observation car painted in State Set green.

Harry Degano Collection

An interesting set of State Cars: all have different names from the common State Cars. The 412 Pullman was named Van Reneselaer instead of California, the 413 Pullman was Star Crest instead of Colorado, and the 416 observation was Vermilion Valley rather than New York. All were names of cars on the *20th Century Limited*.

HANDCARS

James M. Sattler Collection

Here are the four known variations of the handcar, "The item that saved Lionel." The variations are all in the color of the base.

Private Collection

The Santa Claus handcar is normally found with a sack of toys hanging off Santa's back and Mickey Mouse's head sticking out the sack. The normal number is 1105. The 1106 number was used to designate handcars exported to Europe. An indication of how rare this piece is can be found by consulting the Train Collectors Association's fine book *Lionel Trains — Standard of the World, 1900-1943*, which contains the most comprehensive numerical listing of Lionel trains ever made. The number 1106 is omitted.

James M. Sattler Collection

The Donald Duck car with the orange house is the rarest of the Donald Duck handcars.

NEW! ALL-WOOD LIONEL R.R. STRU[CTURES]

NO WAR PRIORITIES! NO LIMIT TO SALES VOLU[ME]

Not construction kits but set-up, completely assembled, all-wood models, ready to use.

● Chalk up another ten-strike for Lionel! With metals becoming increasingly scarce and metal-working machinery mobilized for the war effort, Lionel steps right in to fill the breach with a line of all-wood, all-detailed, scale model railroad structures. *All wood—no metal—not subject to any limitations or restrictions.* Each one a masterpiece of model-making, solidly constructed, tightly assembled and ready to occupy a place of distinction on any model railroad.

1. Freight Station No. 637AW. Typical small-city freight station. Five freight doors slide open and closed. Wide, roof-covered platforms, printed to resemble planking. 8 inches wide, 16 inches long and 7¼ inches high. **Price $5.00**

2. Passenger Station No. 620AW. Combination passenger and express station. At one end of building is a trucking platform with steps on built-up risers. Floor of platform is printed to represent planking. Doors and trim are applied. Station is 8½ inches wide, 12 inches long and 5 inches high. **Price $3.25**

3. Platform Waiting Room No. 623AW. Here's a colorful model that you will surely want for your system. It is perfect for a small town, flag-stop station. If you have a double track line, use it for the w[aiting room...] wide, 11¾ inc[hes...]

4. Interlocki[ng...] of signal tow[er...] colorful with [...] by 6¼ inches, [...]

5. Water To[wer...] standard 50,00[0...] and horizonta[l...] gauge. 6¾ inc[hes...]

Lionel Archives

During World War II Lionel came out with a paper train, which could be made without using metal or other war-priority materials. Lionel also had plans, which reached the prototype stage, for a series of wood buildings. The company had gone as far as printing a flyer for dealers advertising the new buildings, but they never went into production. In addition to the buildings in the flyer at left, Lionel had mockups made of the furniture factory (top) and the restaurant (bottom).

This Nuclear Reactor prototype was never produced, although the 1958 catalog showed a similar dome in the background on page 25. The hand crank on the side works the arm that unloads the car. Inside the dome are a number of revolving lights.

Lionel Archives

Lionel Archives

This was a mock-up of a possible grain elevator which apparently never developed into a final prototype.

CRANE & CARS

The 282 Magnetic Crane prototype. The production model did not have LIONEL written on it, nor was the superstructure black.

Private Collection

Lionel Archives

Lionel Archives

These are prototypes of a car that could be used with the 282 Magnetic Crane. It was a good idea, since it would give the operator something to do with the crane, such as lifting the containers off the flat car and putting them back on. The flat car was a 6511. One of the prototypes had four containers and the other two larger ones. The smaller containers were similar to the prewar LCL containers. They had the same doors that were used on the early milk car. The larger containers had doors from boxcars. Each container, large or small, had a metal washer glued to its top and four pegs on the bottom which fit into holes drilled into the flat cars.

DIESELS

Joseph Siachitano Jr. Collection

A mid-1950s promotional film made by Lionel, featuring a tour of the showroom and factory, showed this prototype black and silver New York Central F-3. None was ever put into production. The engine, because of the type of screens, absence of grab-irons and other details, dates from 1953 or 1954.

Cecil Yother Collection

Prototype for Chicago and North Western 44-Ton switcher that was never produced.

LaRue Shempp Collection

The prototype Union Pacific GP-7 was shown, along with the caboose, at the 1955 toy fair; the engine was also in the 1955 advance catalog. The Lionel model makers used the 1038 number from a real UP engine, although the catalog number was 2028. The engine was never produced, with or without the dynamic brake blister that LaRue Shempp, in whose collection the engine has been for more than 20 years, said was on it when he obtained it.

The 2245 Texas Special prototype had some extra decoration that the production model did not. The stripes on the pilot and "The Texas Special" lettering under the numberboards were excluded from the production run, but both those bits of trim appeared on some of the real trains. The Lionel prototype was painted over a 2355 Western Pacific body.

Lionel Archives

53

Wabash mock-up photographed for the 1957 catalog. The production model GP-7 came with the Wabash flag in gold and red.

Private Collection

James M. Sattler Collection

There are three known variations of the 2028 Pennsylvania Geep: gold (top), yellow (middle), and silver (bottom).

Cecil Yother Collection

The Santa Fe GP-9 prototype.

Howard Godel Collection

It is obvious the boys in the design department were fiddling around a bit with this one. The model, made of plaster, is a hybrid of parts and real life prototypes. It employs some Alco parts, including the fans on the roof, the nose, headlight, sides and trucks. In appearance it is probably closest to the shark-nosed diesels made by Baldwin in the postwar era, but there were no double-ended shark noses made by Baldwin. In his book, *Antique Toy Trains,* author Howard Godel said the Lionel model most resembled a French locomotive. But Godel said later, "I still don't know what it is. I said the engine looked like a model of a French loco, but, having girls on my mind at the time, maybe I was really thinking of a French model."

These photographs of a model of the M-10003 *Streamline* were found in the Lionel archives, but no model was. The *Streamline* the company produced was the M-10000, which came out about the same time as its real life prototype did in 1934. This model is extremely detailed for a Lionel prototype and chances are it was not a Lionel model at all, but one they were studying. But for what? Perhaps they were not even studying it. It might have been a present from the U.P. to some Lionel executive.

Private Collection

In 1957, Lionel re-introduced the Alco diesel. However, what had been a well-constructed and well-running engine, was now a much inferior model (Volume II, page 25). But in the 1957 catalog Lionel used as a photographic model this old Alco, with the good body and die-cast frame, repainted and redecorated with the new 202 designation.

F-3 prototypes on a shelf in the Lionel Archives.

AUTOS & TRUCKS

RC Patrol car

The prototype of the 1981 Lionel Remote Control police car, like the Turbo-Z Camaro, was built to 1/16 scale. It originally was to have been produced with the Fundimensions name on it. A year was spent on its design and another two years on its development. Before coming out with it, however, a market research study was made. Four-hundred people were shown pictures of remote control cars at a shopping mall. Two-hundred people were shown the car with the Fundimensions name on it and the other two-hundred were shown a picture with the Lionel name on it. Both groups of people were asked the same question about what they perceived as attributes of the car. It turned out that the people who saw the picture of the car with "Lionel" on it rated the car higher all around than those who saw the car with "Fundimensions" on it. The surveyed people said the Lionel car looked stronger, faster, and connoted more value than the other car.

Turbo Z/TNT Camaro.

Private Collection

This is the only time the 6414 Auto-Loader was known to have green cars, which makes an extremely common item interesting. The item was discovered in the U.S. Embassy in Belegrade, Yugoslavia.

Prototype for piggy-back car with Sears trailers, which, through 1981 had not been produced.

Lionel Archives

In the years following World War II, Lionel had plans to diversify, although because of various financial reasons they did not until the post-Joshua Cowen era of the 1960s. Some products they had developed included room air-conditioners, motorized bicycles, and wooden toys of the later Playschool and Fischer-Price variety. The Sunoco truck is one of the prototype, high-quality wooden toys made by Lionel in the late 1940s but never produced.

Lionel Archives

Private Collection

Lionel offered the "Famous Lionel Racing Electric Automobiles" in its 1915 catalog. (see Volume I, page 106). A few cars are still around, but a complete set, boxed and including the fragile paper Start-Finish sign, is almost unique.

STEAM ENGINES

LaRue Shempp Collection

This was a chrome-plated 1666 made for Charles Giaimo, a Lionel executive. Inside the cab is a worn inscription that contains the year presented to Giaimo, 1946, and the words, "... Mr. Giaimo's desk at Lionel Plant."

A prototype for a General-type engine by Fundimensions, which as the book went to print had not yet been produced.

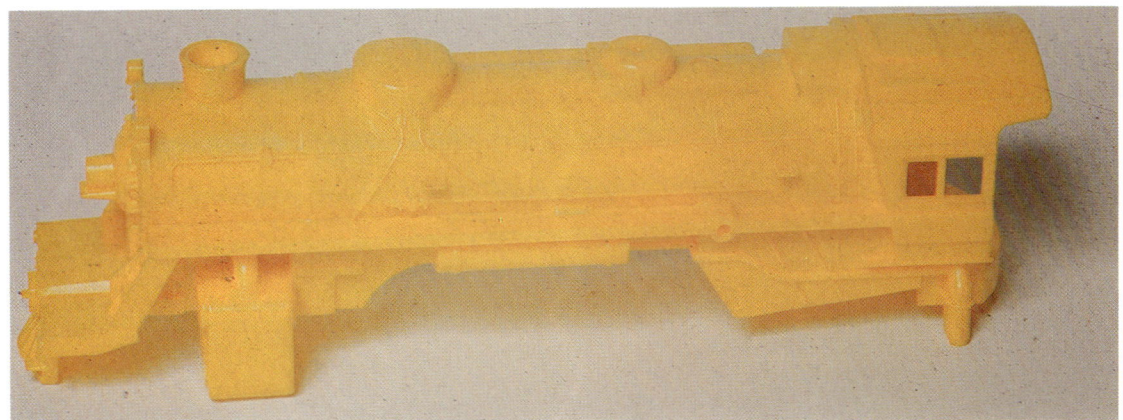

When an injection molding machine is fired-up for a run, about 150 shells, or shots, are sent through for practice. This purges the machine of any plastic left over from the previous run. In 1970, when the molding machine was fired up to make a run of bodies for the 8043 Nickel Plate small steamer, there was still some yellow plastic left over from the last time it had been used in New Jersey. A few yellow boilers were therefore produced and the one pictured, according to Lee Jones, who was then manager of manufacturing for Lionel, was the first plastic train part to come out of a machine at Mount Clemens, Michigan.

Lionel Archives

Much tinkering was going on when this piece was put together. What the engineers were striving for is unclear. The loco has a brass cast boiler, a Pennsy turbine boiler front, the cowcatcher and smokestack from a 2026, and the drivers from a 221. The idea, whatever it was, apparently never caught on.

LaRue Shempp Collection

When Lionel re-released the 773 Hudson in 1964, there were several changes made on the engine, including the lettering and an absence of slide valve guides on the steam chest (see Volume II, page 54). There also, apparently, were contemplated changes that were experimented with on a prototype but never mass-produced. These included the red marker lights shown in this photograph and a red light located underneath the cab which simulated the glow from a firebox, similar to the light on the 226E (Volume I, page 90).

This Fundimensions prototype is slightly different than the production model. The production model had an all-blue cab and a yellow stripe on the running board, without the yellow stripe or patch below the cab windows. The number on the production model was yellow and was changed to 8008, but the 8006 number did appear on a limited-run Silver Shadow steamer made for J. C. Penney.

Lionel introduced its F-3s at the New York Toy Fair in 1948. Displayed were the New York Central and Santa Fe engines, but to show off its new twin-motored insides, the company made some clear plastic bodies. All of these clear plastic display models might have had Santa Fe markings on them but some collectors believe there were three different types of display bodies, and they are represented on this page. Although admittedly speculative, the belief of these collectors is that some engines had no markings, some had nose markings and the GM logo, and some had nose markings, war bonnet striping and GM logo. Those who dispute the three-types-of-trim theory, think all the engines had full markings which have worn off through the years. The plastic itself was clearer when new but has yellowed with age.

DISPLAY ENGINES

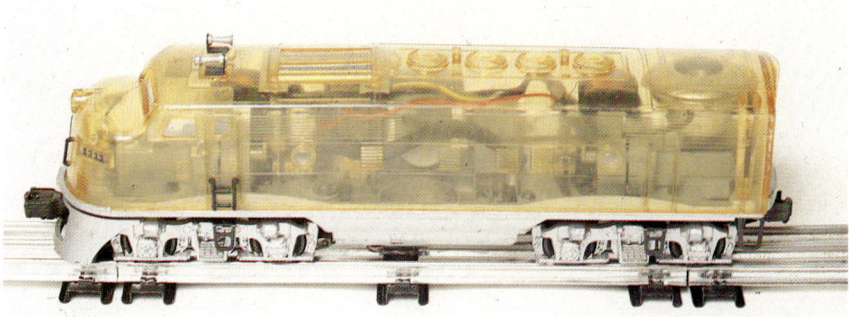

TRACK

Lionel Archives

Track was something with which Lionel almost always experimented. This track was from the early 50s, at a time when the company wanted more realism. The sections are all-metal and the roadbed is raised to a hump between the rails. The third rail is placed at the high point of the hump, disguised as part of the roadbed. The whole concept is quite similar to the Marklin HO track. The Lionel track was handsome but undoubtedly would have been expensive to produce.

Lionel Archives

The wood prototype for the 072 switch.

Lionel Archives

The wood prototype for the 022 switch.

TIMER

James M. Sattler Collection

Rear View

Lionel had progressed close to the production stage of this automatic timing device, which was designated No. 26 Timer. It was designed for use on dealer displays, not for retail sales. It could control the operation of a number of accessories, including two 313 Bascule Bridges, simultaneously or in sequence. The accessories could be set to go up and down or back and forth or on and off at predetermined times as a train made its way along the display layout.

ACCESSORIES

Lionel Archives

This prototype for a lighthouse accessory uses a bulb that is the same dimpled type used on the Floodlight accessory.

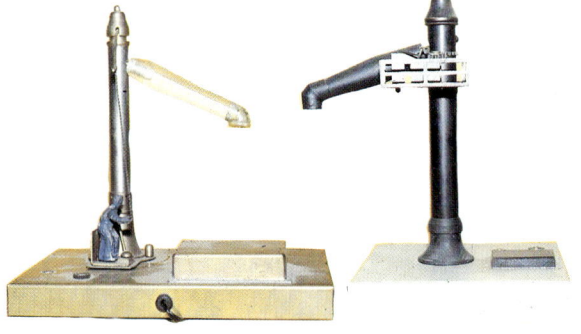

These water columns were never produced. On real trains such columns were used to fill tenders from underground water tanks.

Richard Cowan Collection

The 57 Lamp Post is usually found in orange and the street names are usually Main Street and Broadway — 21st Street, 42nd Street and Fifth Avenue were not main drags, so to speak, in Lionelville, even though the Lionel offices in New York City were once located on 21st Street.

Lionel Archives

An accessory designed to unload crates from a car, it was probably designed in the mid-50s and rejected because of the cost. The unloading platform worked very much like the Fork Lift and Saw Mill accessories. The car operated like the Barrel Car, with a vibrating action moving the crates onto the platform.

Lionel Archives

This accessory, probably designed in the mid to late 50s, was Lionel's attempt to compete with American Flyer's 594 Animated Track Gang accessory. The workmen were operated by a solenoid. When the button was pressed, the workers slid out over the track and when the button was released they scurried back to get out of the way of the approaching train. The generator from the searchlight served as power source.

69

TOY SHOW MOCK-UPS

Lionel did not always do things the same way every time when it came to prototypes. Sometimes the prototype was used for the picture in the catalog and sometimes a handmade mock-up of the prototype was made and *that* was photographed for the catalog. Sometimes the prototype was sent to the toy fairs for exhibition and sometimes not. Instead, they might make several mock-ups and send them to different toy fairs and showrooms. Such was the case with the mock-ups on these pages. Perhaps as many as six of each of them were made and shown around the country. Each, though, was made by hand at Lionel, and each is a great prize for a collector.

Howard Godel Collection

Howard Godel Collection

Howard Godel Collection

Howard Godel Collection

71

IDEAS FROM MOUNT CLEMENS

Lionel Archives

This zip code car was contemplated as some kind of bicentennial car in 1976 but the idea never fully developed.

Lionel Archives

The Tootsie Pop Drops tanker was planned for the 1981 line but it was not made.

This was the original prototype of the 5705 Ball Reefer. After Lionel decided to make a car with the Ball name on it, they made a routine request for permission from Ball. Lionel had designed the graphics according to the Ball logo and its own designers' imaginations. Lionel was not aware that the Ball company once had their own railroad cars back in the 1920s. When the Ball people saw the fanciful Lionel design they sent Lionel a photograph of the real Ball car and told them what the colors were. Lionel had already taken a picture of its first design for the catalog, so the manufactured item differed greatly from the car in the catalog. A similar thing happened at Lionel in 1979, when Lionel had a Kraft car designed and photographed for the catalog before finding out from Kraft that permission to use its name had been withdrawn.

Lionel Archives

9700 Southern prototype, was produced with different graphics after Southern changed theirs.

IDEAS FROM IRVINGTON

Lionel Archives

A fine item that was never produced, this molten steel dump car, would have made a good postwar cousin to the Standard Gauge coal train. An 0-4-0 switcher pulling six of these molten steel cars with a red caboose at the end would have made a striking set. The prototype was made of solid brass and designed to operate like the ore unloading car.

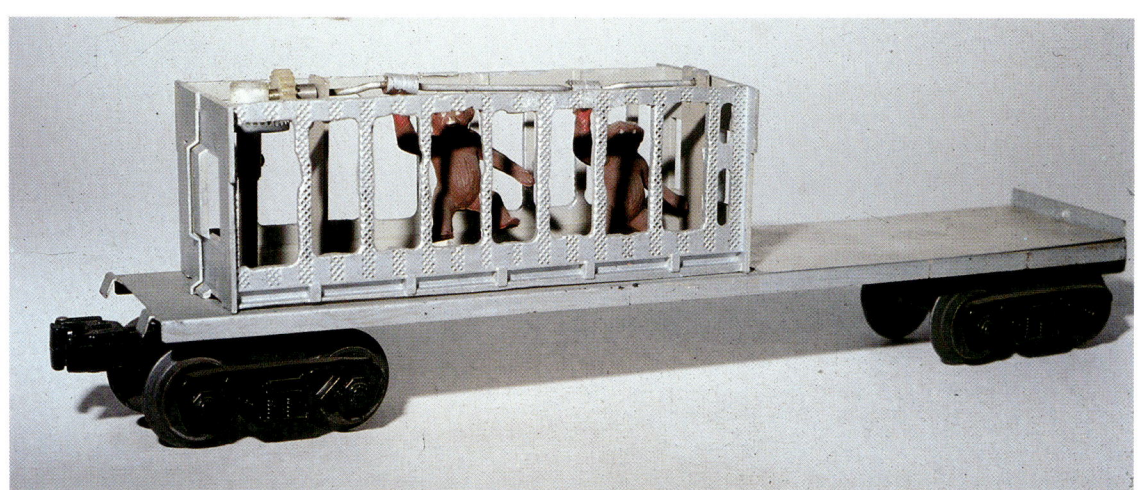

Lionel Archives

Volume IV in the Lionel Collector Series contained a picture of the "Jumping Gorilla" car without the cage surrounding the gorillas. On the author's last trip to the archives they found the cage and placed it over the gorillas.

Lionel Archives

This Burlington reefer was never produced, and, in fact, even as a prototype it was not complete. It was a painted-over Santa Fe reefer and was decaled on one side only.

Lionel Archives

A prototype transformer, which was never produced, was bigger, at 400 watts, than any Lionel ever made.

Lionel Archives

Prototype for Seabrook Farms boxcar. Never produced.

LaRue Shempp Collection

LaRue Shempp Collection

MORE GG-1's AND OTHER ELECTRICS

Joshua Cowen had the nickel-plated GG-1 made for LaRue Shempp of Williamsport, Pennsylvania, in 1950. Shempp once mentioned to Cowen that a nickel-plated GG-1 would "dress up" his Congressional set, and, to his surprise, Shempp received one. "Keep me in mind if you ever want to trade that No. 1 trolley of yours," Cowen said. Shempp has one of the few No. 1 trolleys in existence. Repeated polishing wore the yellow stripes and lettering off the nickel-plated GG-1. Bill Vagell, the top Lionel dealer on the East Coast during the postwar boom days, lived in Garfield, New Jersey, only a few miles from Lionel's Irvington factory. He was on good terms with the people there and often had them make him custom items. In 1963 Vagell plated the copper and brass GG-1s (left) himself, then took them to the Lionel factory, where they were hot-stamped and lined. These one-of-a-kind items were sold to LaRue Shempp. Shempp lacquered his gold and copper GG-1s, thus preserving their markings.

Private Collection

Bill Vagell had eight GG-1s painted black and then had Lionel letter and stripe them. He did it after some collectors claimed that Lionel once mistakenly made a few black GG-1s. Vagell always said the disputed color was a very dark green. "I got so mad at everybody calling them black that in 1963 I took eight GG-1s of my own, painted them black and brought them back to Lionel..." said Vagell (Volume II, page 37).

LaRue Shempp Collection

The original GG-1, the 2332, had only one motor. Twin motors were introduced in 1950, with the 2330, but for the prototype model, Lionel merely used the shell from an old 2332.

Lionel Archives

In the summer of 1980 Lionel collector Stewart Roberts of Columbus, Ohio, after elaborate preparations and several tries, managed, with the assistance of several other collectors, to get an O gauge train of 752 Lionel boxcars pulled around a 2,000-foot loop of track by 32 Lionel engines, thirty of which were Penn Central GG-1s. The feat made the *Guinness Book of Records,* which is interested in weird things like that. Although a publicity stunt, Lionel people are proud of the feat, and so is Roberts, who worked very hard to achieve it.

James M. Sattler Collection

The Pennsylvania rectifier prototype has hand-painted yellow stripes and box, and the lettering and numbers are hand-cut decals.

Gaetano J. D'Angelo Collection

In 1956 Lionel made a few 2350 New Havens with special LIONEL lettering for display at various toy shows and showrooms.

James M. Sattler Collection

Lionel's 1956 catalog shows the 2350 New Haven rectifier with the stripes painted across the door jambs. This is the mock-up used for that catalog photograph. The production models had the stripe interrupted by the jambs.

Richard Cowan Collection

The 607 green Pullman is not often found with Illinois Central markings. It's usually Lionel Lines. The 252 engine in front of it is also unusual in that it has orange beading at the bottom of the cab. Most do not. Both items are probably from a Department Store Special set.

Richard Cowan Collection

The olive 254 with red trim, and the olive 605 series cars make up one of the hardest to find cataloged sets of the prewar era. It was catalogued in 1931 and 1932.

Private Collection

The 1912 with thin rims normally came in dark olive green, not black as it is here.

81

MORE STANDARD GAUGE

Private Collection

This is the rarest and most desired of the Lionel trolleys: the number 9, nine-window version with twin motors.

Private Collection

This 219 Crane has the cab window and the door reversed from their normal positions.

Private Collection

Lionel made a few Standard Gauge trolleys for the Maryland Electrical Supply Co. and named them after trolley routes in Baltimore. Among those were the No. 1 Curtis Bay and 100 Linden Ave. These trolleys were usually stamped "Electric Rapid Transit."

Private Collection

Private Collection

This 402 in mustard is another paint sample.
There is a set of 419-series cars that match.

The Macy's Special Set headed by a red 10 is very rare. It was a fine looking set, but when seen nowadays it is usually — and understandably — beat up. This one is in mint condition with the box. They don't get much better than this.

Private Collection

This is a 408E paint sample.

Private Collection

The 408E loco and 419 Combine Car in turquoise were color samples made by Lionel, which in the 1920s often tested one or two with non-production colors to see how they looked.

2-7/8-INCH GAUGE

James M. Sattler Collection

This is what is believed to be the earliest wooden gondola made by the Lionel Manufacturing Company of New York. It is finished in red, rather than the brown of the second series of wooden gondolas made in 1902.

James M. Sattler Collection

The 100 Electric and the 500 Motorized Derrick, two of the earliest cars made by Lionel, were probably only produced in the year 1903.

Private Collection

The few 2⅞-inch Gauge 100 Trolleys that are known to exist are stamped "B&O No. 5." This one must have been a department store special from the St. Louis area.

Private Collection

The 2⅞-inch Gauge Converse Trolley and 800 Boxcar, shown with the 340 Bridge accessory.

ROLLING STOCK PROTOTYPES

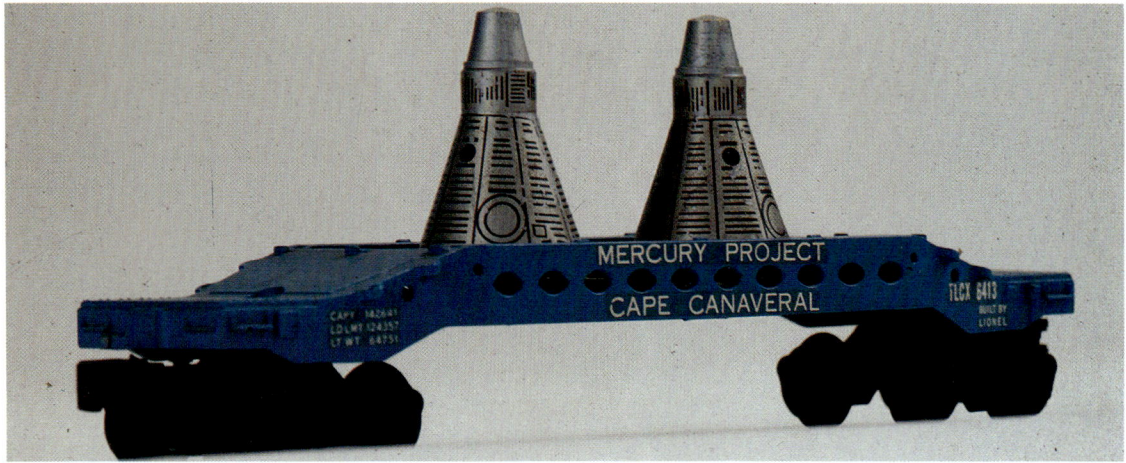

Cecil Yother Collection

The prototype for the 6413 Mercury Capsule Carrying Car has pen-sketched wood models for capsules; the production models had plastic capsules.

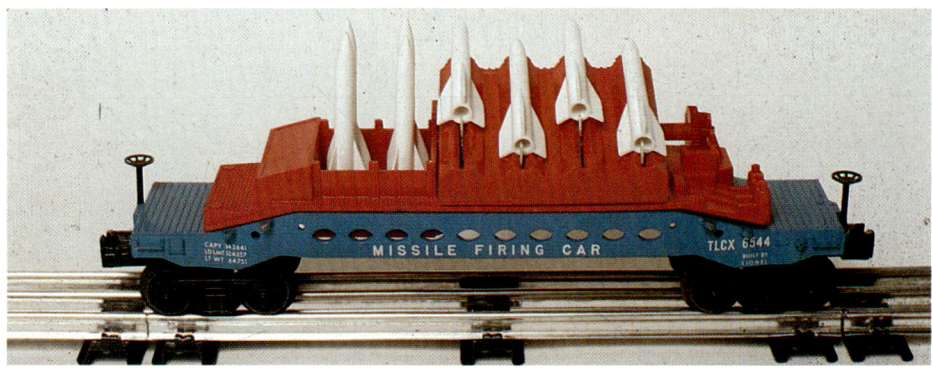

Private Collection

6544 Missile Firing Car prototype. Production model has gray missile firing mechanism.

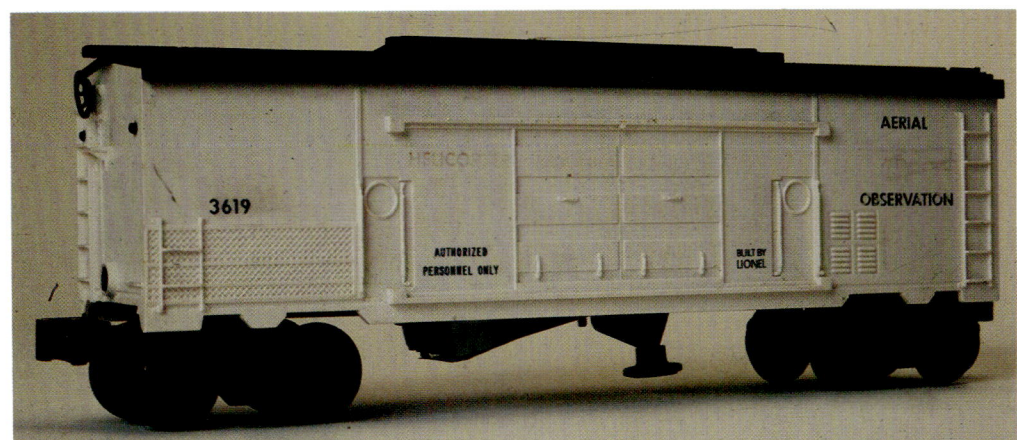

James M. Sattler Collection

The prototype for the yellow and black 3619 aerial observation car.

James M. Sattler Collection

The prototype for the 3419 Operating Helicopter car is unpainted gray plastic and has no numbers or letters. The helicopter is identical to the production model.

James M. Sattler Collection

The 6356 Bi-level Stock Car was produced with yellow body and black letters, not with this rare white body.

James M. Sattler Collection

An early mock-up of the 3376 Giraffe car. The car was painted on the top and sides only and did not operate as yet. The giraffe's head and neck were screwed into the metal base. The car had none of the moving parts of the production model.

James M. Sattler Collection

The prototype for the blue and white hydraulic platform maintenance car.

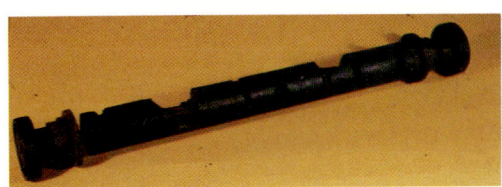

Lionel Archives

In the postwar era Lionel used a printing machine to mark their rolling stock. This roller bar from those days — now they have much more sophisticated stamping machines — contains various road names, including Rock Island, Burlington and Pennsylvania, which are discernible upon close-up inspection but not in this picture.

James M. Sattler Collection

This mock-up of the 3356 Operating Horse car was used as a model for the artist's rendering in the 1959 catalog. It had white lettering instead of the production yellow.

James M. Sattler Collection

The prototype of the 6050 Savings Bank car had different style lettering than the production model.

Lionel Archives

The prototype of the 9233 Depressed Center Transformer car. Although the number 9388 appears on the prototype, it was changed along with the colors (to brown and red) on the production model.

ROLLING STOCK COLOR VARIATIONS

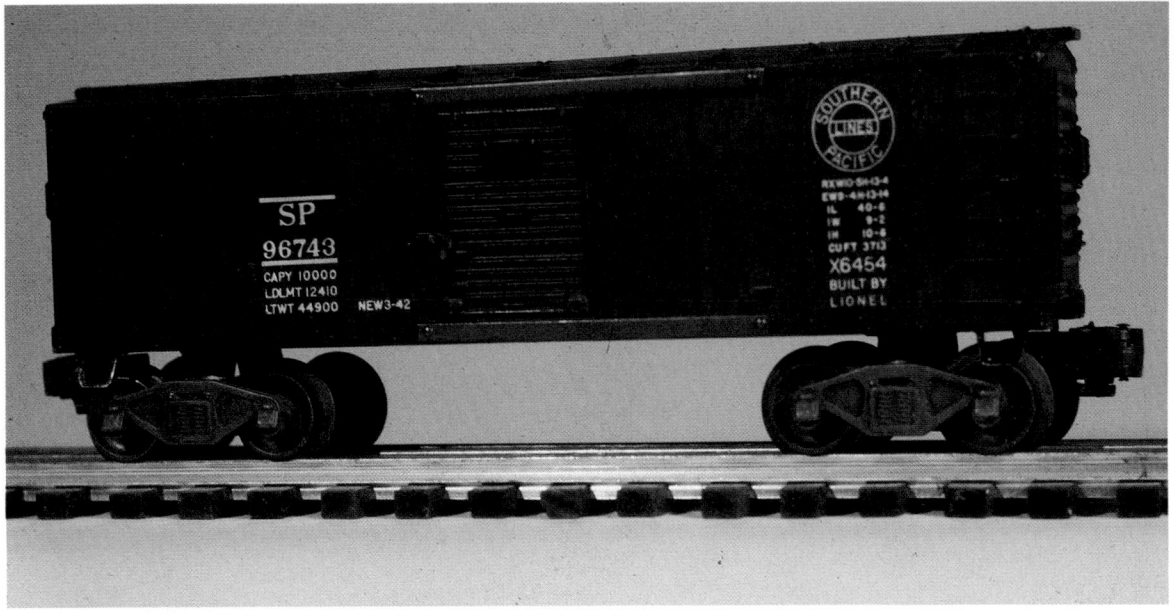

Harry Degano Collection

No one had ever heard of this car, made about 1950, coming in black. But it did at least once. Usual color was Tuscan.

The 3484 AT&SF operating boxcar has never before been seen in this shade of orange, but always in a lighter orange.

James M. Sattler Collection

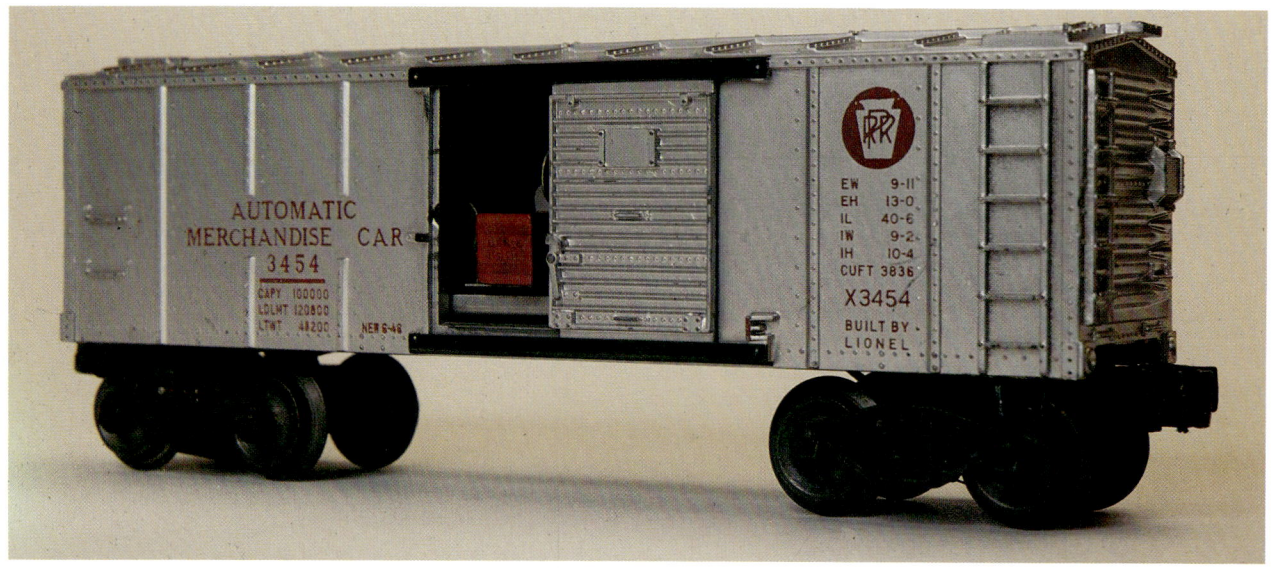

James M. Sattler Collection

The 3454 Pennsylvania Operating Car with red lettering instead of blue.

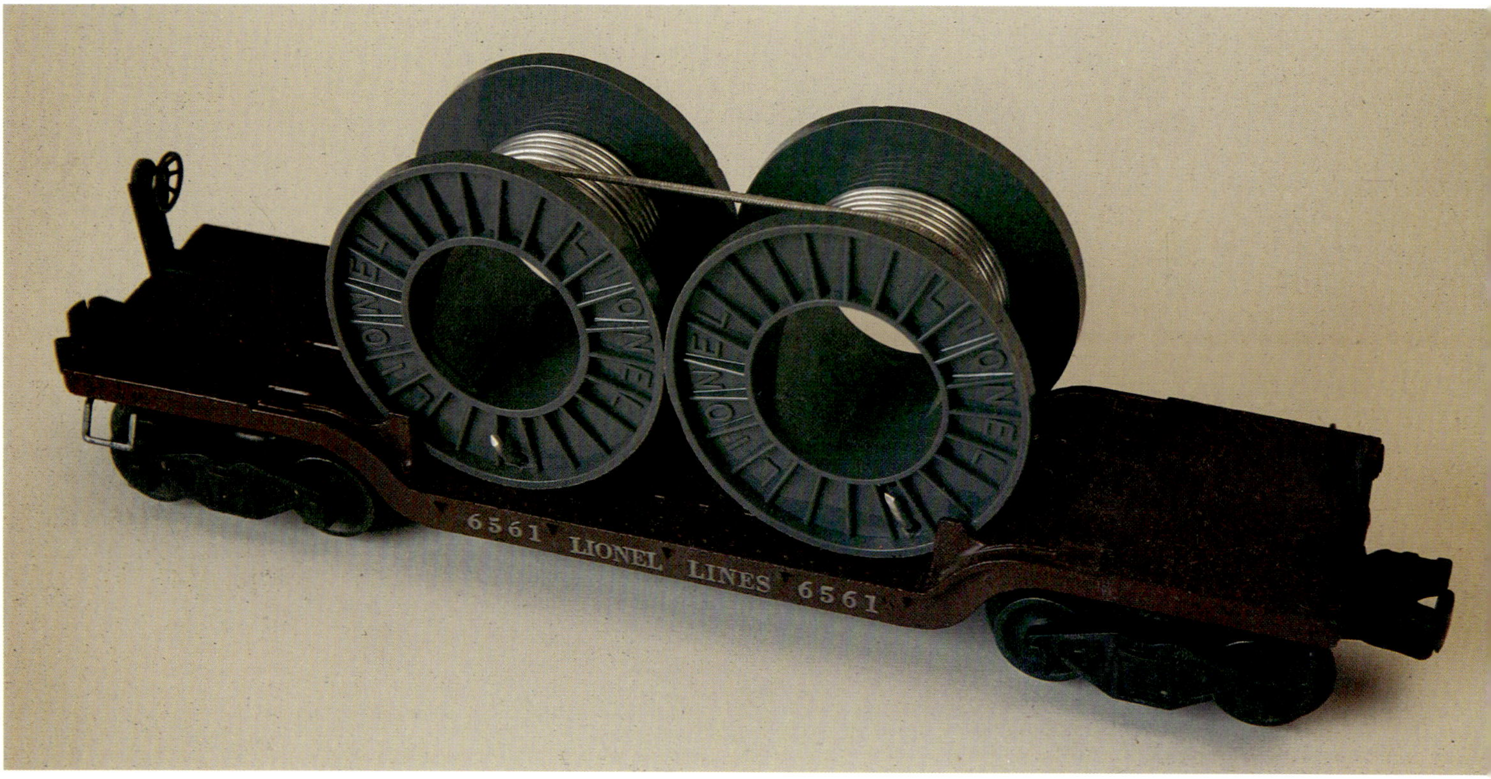

James M. Sattler Collection

6562 Cable Car in rare brown variation with silver lettering.

James M. Sattler Collection

The 6462 New York Central gondola is perhaps one-of-a-kind, on cars with brakewheels. It has never been seen in orange, only black and red. (see Volume II, page 92).

The 3484 Pennsylvania Operating Boxcar with rare cream-gold lettering is in the front and the same car with the common white lettering is in the rear.

95

The 6014 Wix boxcar, the hardest to find of the postwar scout-type boxcars, was made usually in cream. This one is snow white.

James M. Sattler Collection

Harry Degano Collection

The 6636 Alaska hopper with white lettering rather than yellow.

This was one of several colors tried before Lionel settled on the pale green version that was manufactured.

Harry Degano Collection

In 1966 Lionel made an orange Erie-style caboose for the Train Collectors Association. The production run Erie caboose was red, but a few orange cabooses were stamped with Erie markings prior to the run of the TCA caboose.

Harry Degano Collection

The 6417-51 gray Lehigh Valley with blue lettering rather than red.

James M. Sattler Collection

6427 Virginian caboose with white rather than yellow lettering.

Harry Degano Collection

The 6417-51 was most common in gray, unusual in Tuscan with white lettering, very rare with silver lettering. Harry Degano also has a Tuscan 6417-51 with gold lettering.

PASSENGER CARS

Lionel Archives

Lionel decided to paint its aluminum passenger cars in 1980, but since the aluminum cars had never been painted before, there was a question as to whether the paint would adhere to the aluminum. A sample was painted in Daylight colors. It worked fine. At that point Lionel planned to make the Southern Pacific Daylight its first passenger set with painted aluminum cars, but as it turned out the Powhatan Arrow was the first set with painted cars.

A more finished paint sample, shown in the lower photograph, has the Daylight stripes above and below the windows. This sample eventually became the first full-blown Daylight prototype passenger car. For the Daylight engine Lionel used the Berkshire with side skirting added and a new nose, made from a new plastic tool. The tender was the same small plastic coal tender used with other steamers. Making a tool for the Vandy-type tender used by the real Daylight was too expensive, the Lionel cost-analysts decided.

The smoke unit for the Daylight engine was the same that was developed for the Norfolk and Western. The unit is a very efficient one, putting out a great deal of smoke from chemical drops, which were basically mineral oil. The engineer on the Norfolk project, Jim Van Syckle, thought it would be good to have smoke coming out of the pistons, too. He attached a tube to the smoke unit and ran it to the sides. Old Lionel used smoke pellets, which were developed by a Lionel chemist, Mario Mazzoni.

Lionel Archives

Richard Cowan Collection

The Manhattan car numbered 2624 is the most rare of the Irvington cars. Six are known to exist. The common Manhattan number was 2623. The 2624 number was supposed to have been given to an observation car in 1941, but Lionel never did make one.

Lionel Archives

This is the wood mock-up for the passenger car Lionel-Fundimensions introduced in 1973. See page 95 in Volume IV for more details about the development of this model.

Lou Redman Collection

These cars appear to be hand-made pre-production models with die-cast roof, vestibule and door handles. The combine car has the 611 number that was omitted from the 610-series cars of 1926, which contained a 610 Pullman and 612 observation. But these cars are the style of the 613-series of 1931, not the earlier 610-series.

SKETCHES & DRAWINGS

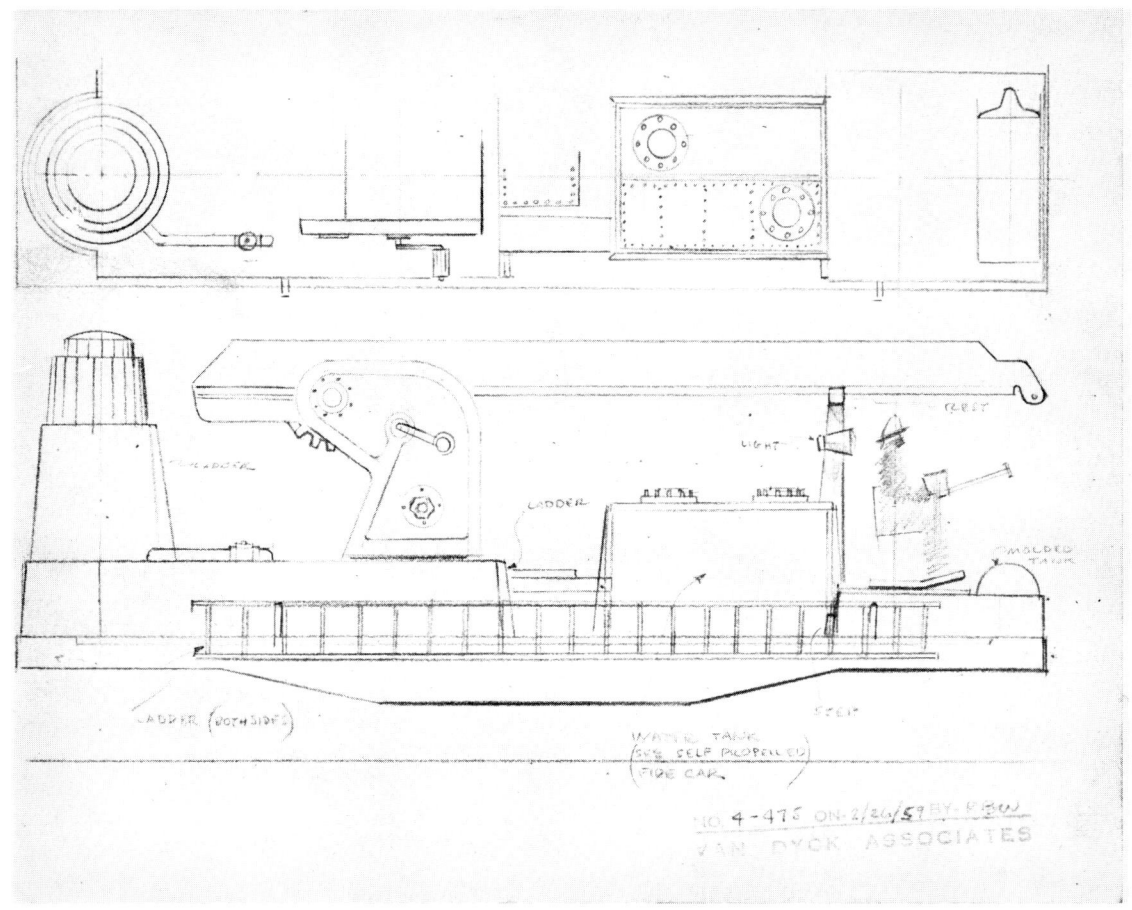

Lionel's chief engineer, Joe Bonanno, kept a file of drawings that were made for hundreds of different items. Many were produced, many were not. It is fascinating to look at the drawings because they show the progression of an idea from its rough beginnings to its rather thorough conclusion. Space does not allow for the publication of all the drawings in Joe Bonanno's "idea book," but these last 16 pages show some of them.

As explained on page 4, Lionel kept on retainer a designer named Peter Van Dyke. Van Dyke, working with Bonanno and his assistants, would make quick preliminary drawings based on ideas the engineers had. These drawings were later refined and as this section shows, often became quite detailed, although the marketed products were usually different in several ways.

This page shows one of the drawings for what eventually became the 3517 operating fireman and ladder car. Overleaf is a picture of a proposed locomotive cab. The child would look at the screen on which the simulated view of the engineer would be projected. The drawings in this section are not captioned. For the most part they are self-explanatory. For those things that were not manufactured and whose purpose is not quite clear, the reader is as capable as the authors of discerning what the purpose might have been.

NO. 4-531 ON 8-25-59 BY C
VAN DYCK ASSOCIATES

NO. 4-537 ON 8-25-59 BY C
VAN DYCK ASSOCIATES

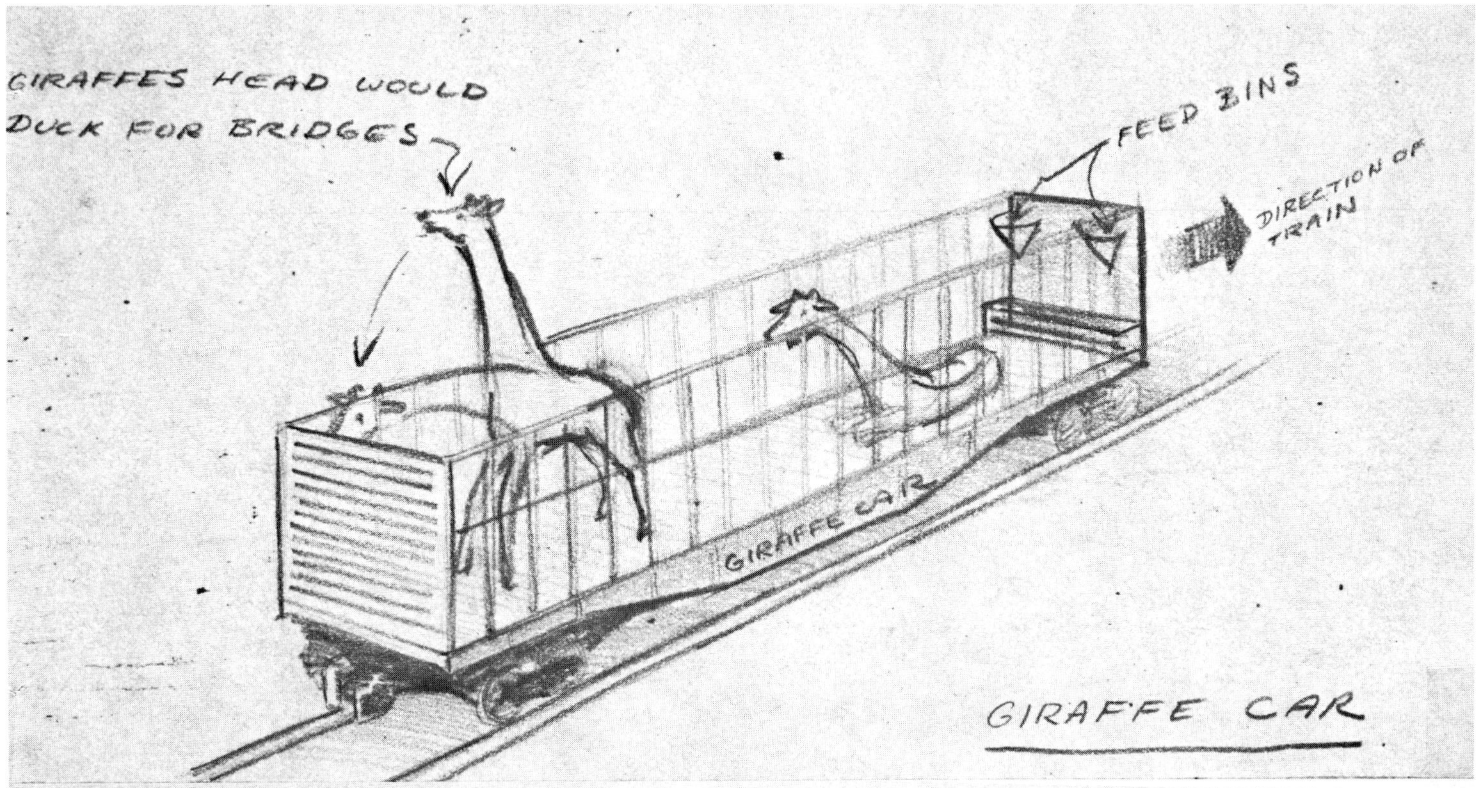

GIRAFFES HEAD WOULD
DUCK FOR BRIDGES

GIRAFFE CAR

1) HAVE MONKEY ON TRAPEZE SO AS TO SWING WHEN TRAIN MOVES.
2) HAVE 2 OR 3 SECTIONS WITH DIFFERENT KINDS OF MONKEYS.

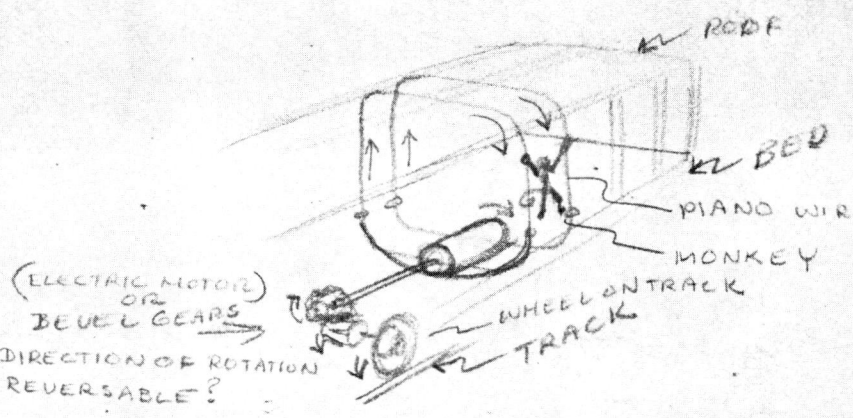

MAKE SOME BARS OF PIANO WIRE SO AS TO BE FLEXIBLE ENOUGH TO ROTATE AS SHOW ABOVE MONKEY WOULD APPEAR TO CLIMB UP AND DOWN

MONKEY CAR

NO. 4-5/9 OR 7/7/59 BY ℗
VAN DYCK ASSOCIATES

NO. 4-518 ON BY
VAN DYCK ASSOCIATES

MONKEY SWINGS ON TRAPEE
MONKEY MOVES UP & DOWN BARS

LCF
LIONEL ZOO
NO. 4-526 ON 8/6/59 BY
VAN DYCK ASSOCIATES

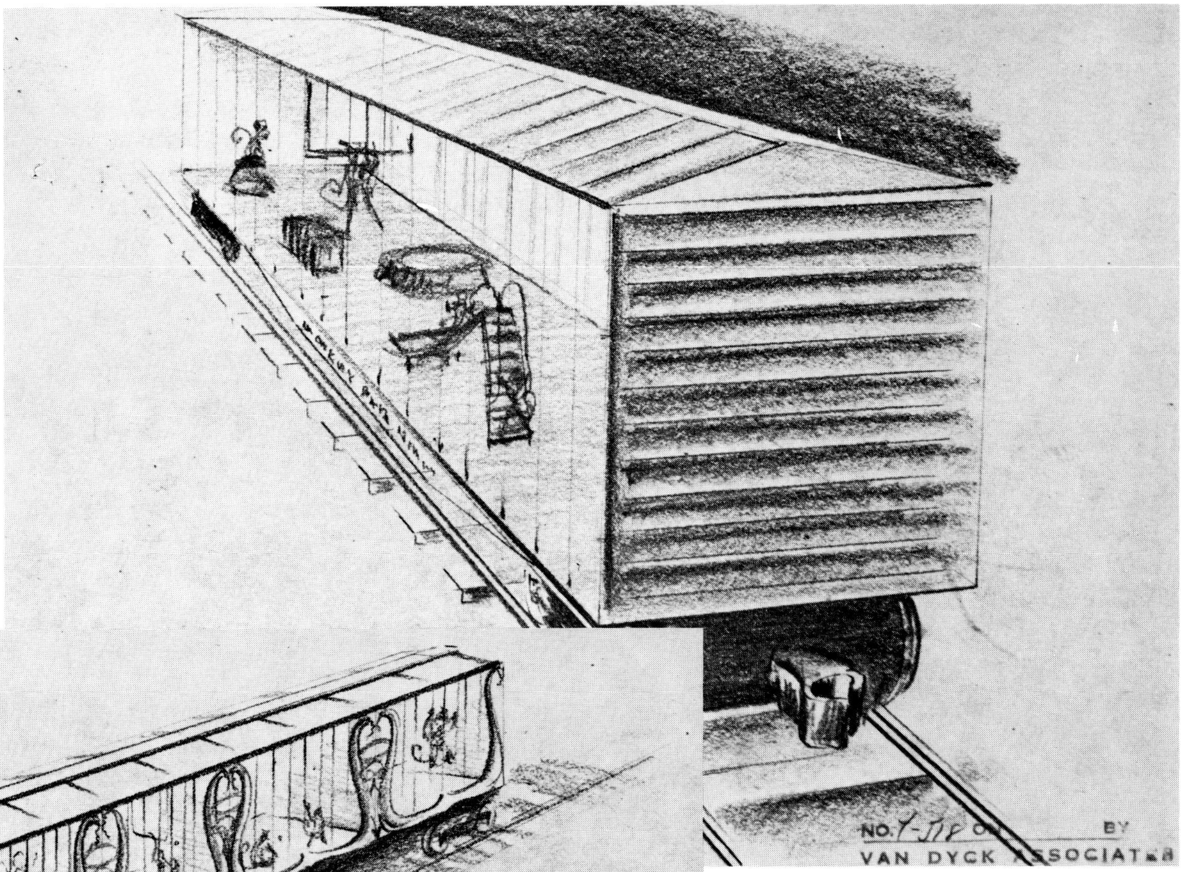

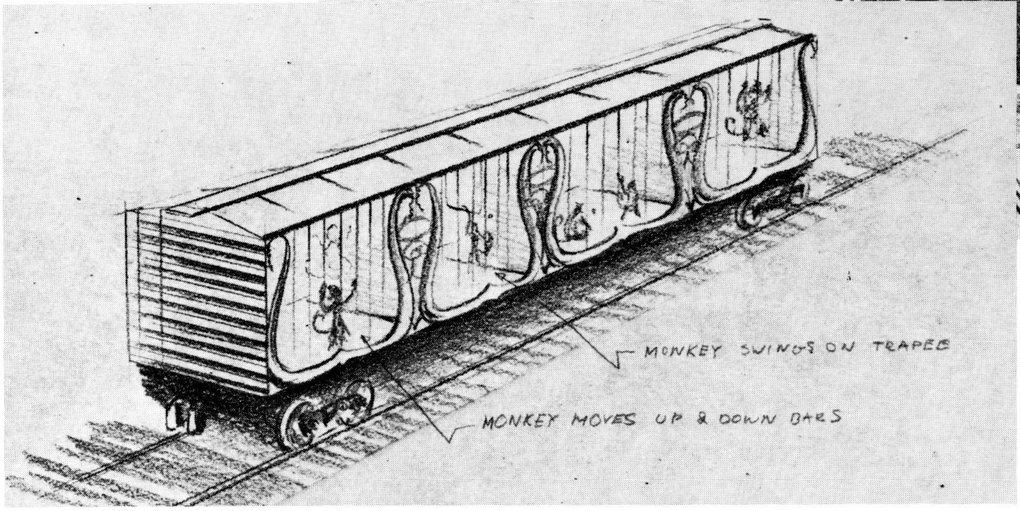

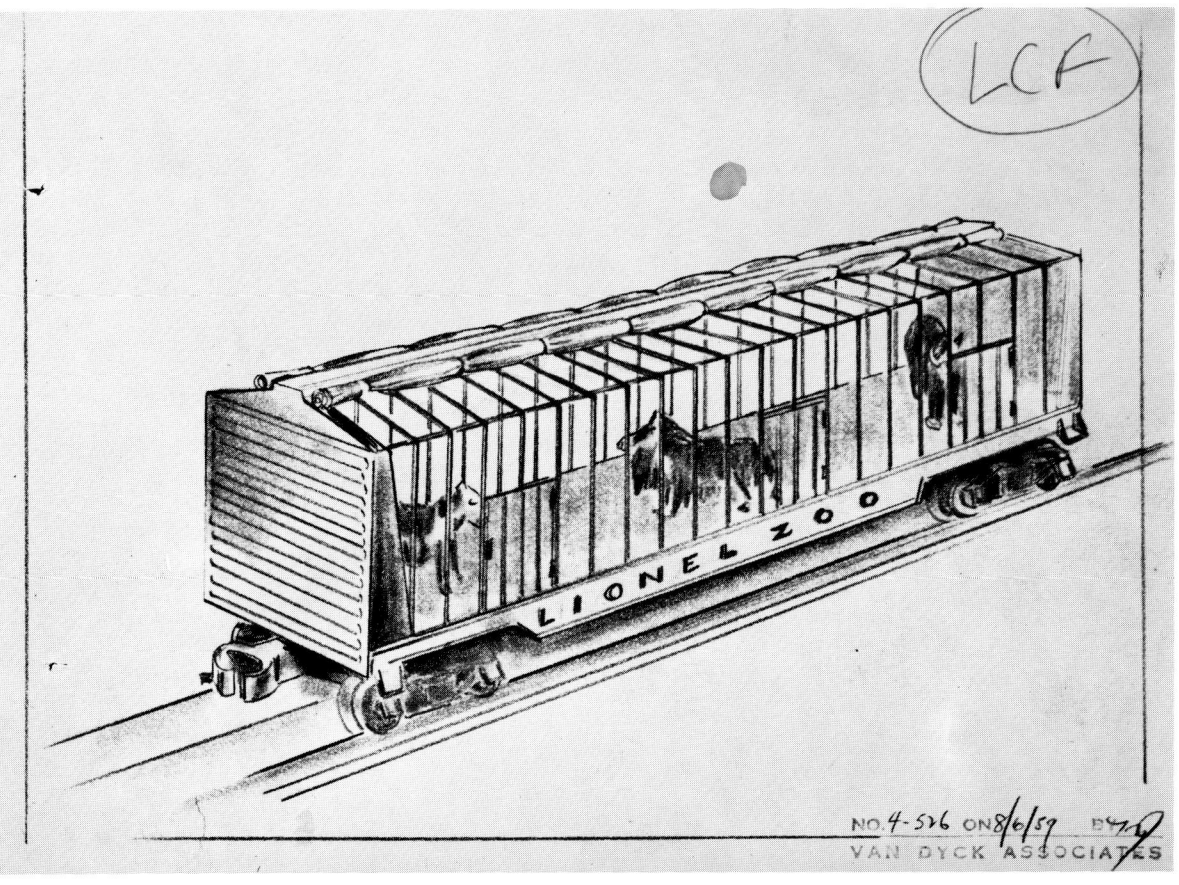

DANGER

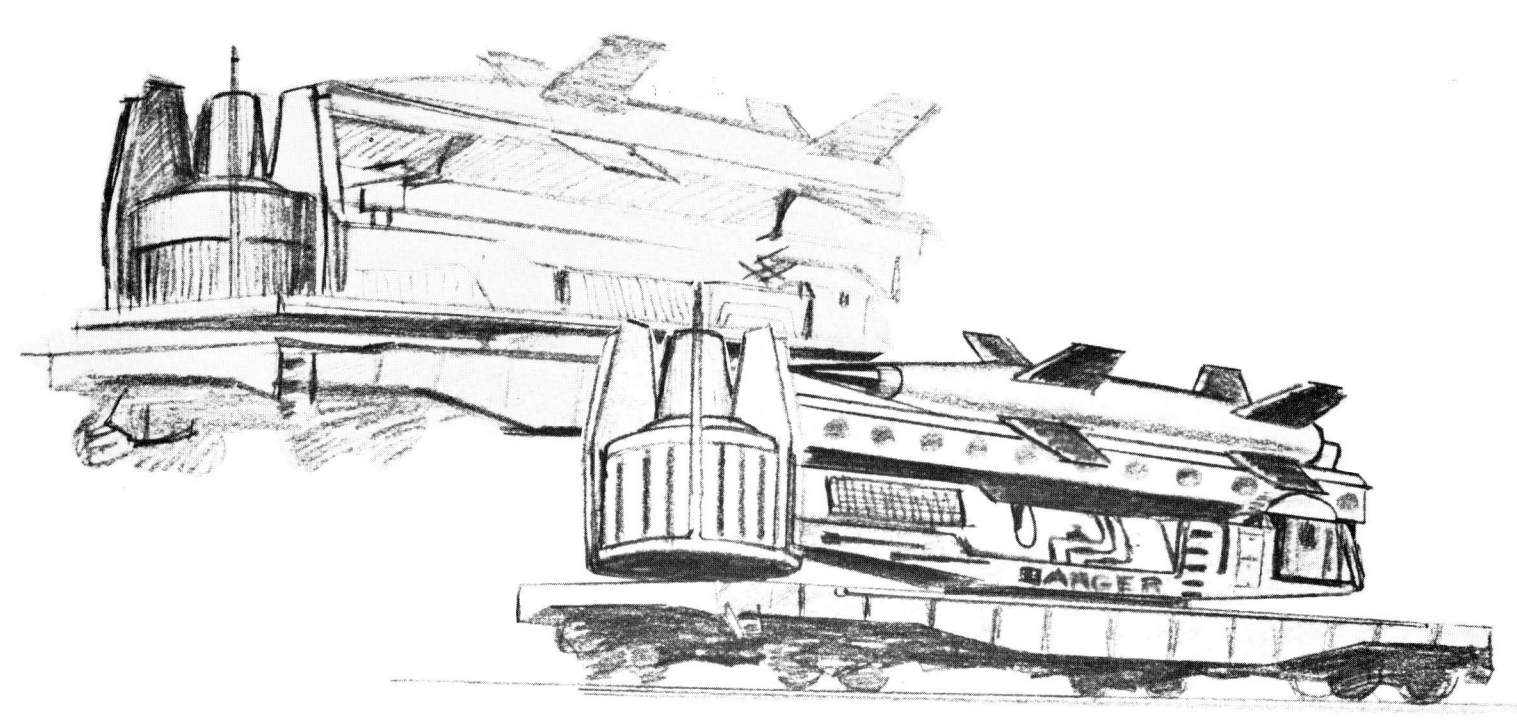

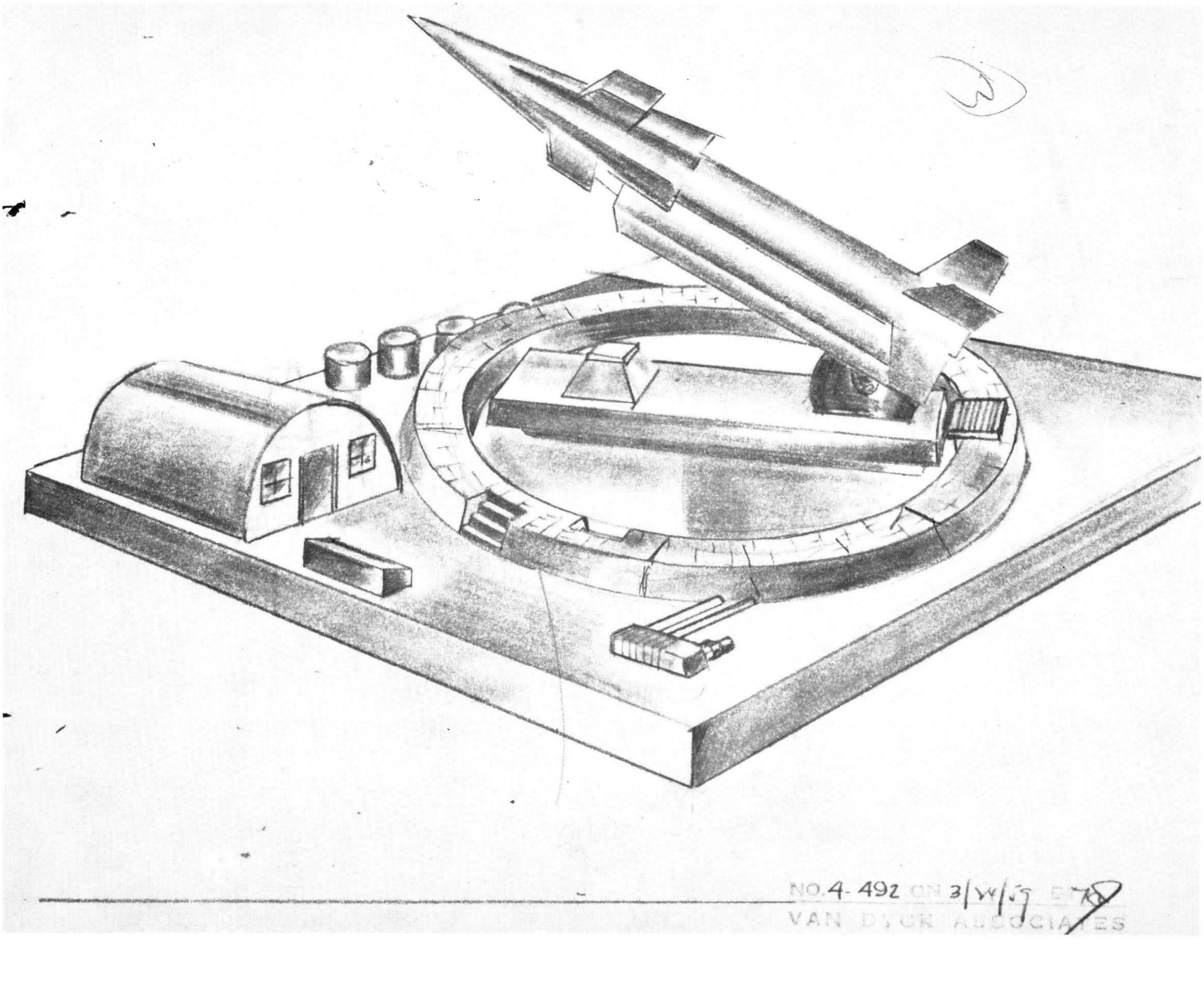
NO. 4-492 ON
VAN DYCK ASSOCIATES

CEMENT TOGETHER HERE
NO CLAMP RINGS PLEASE !!

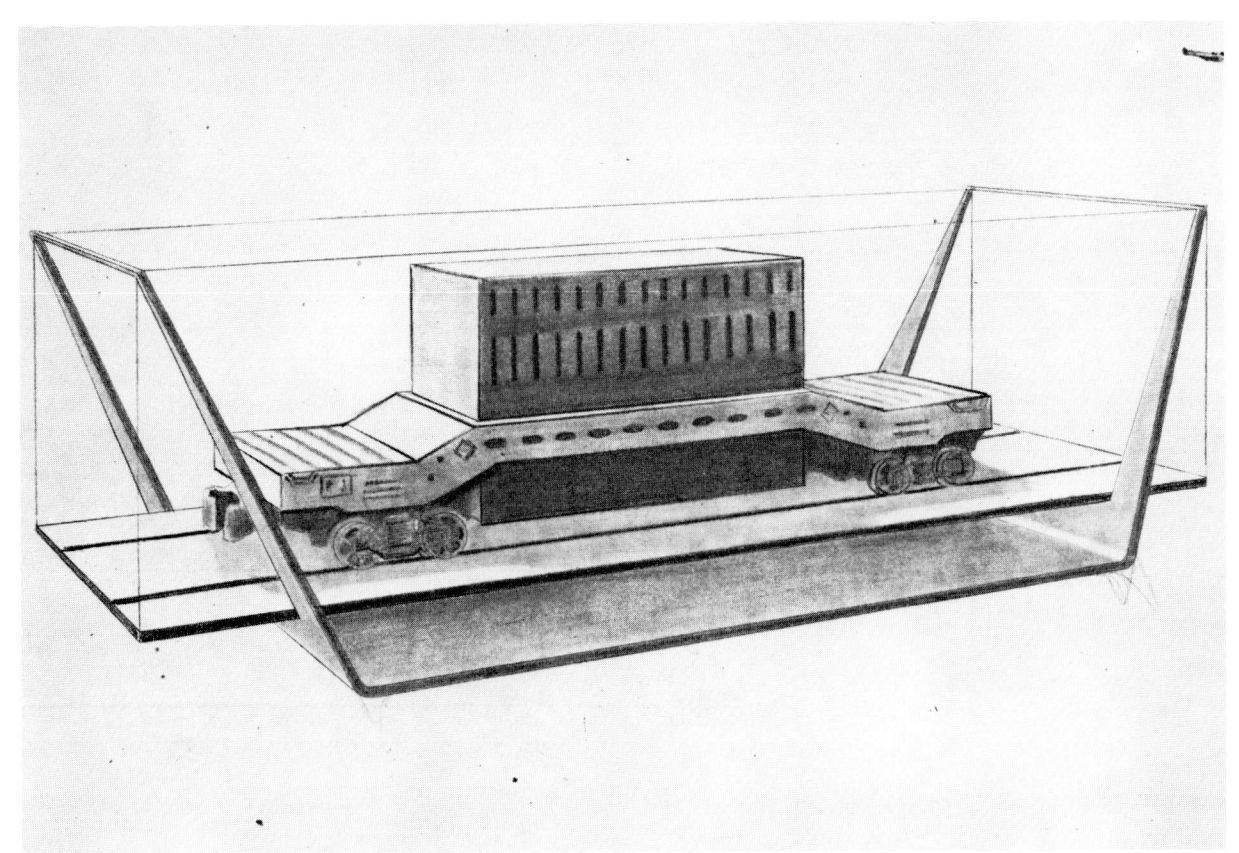

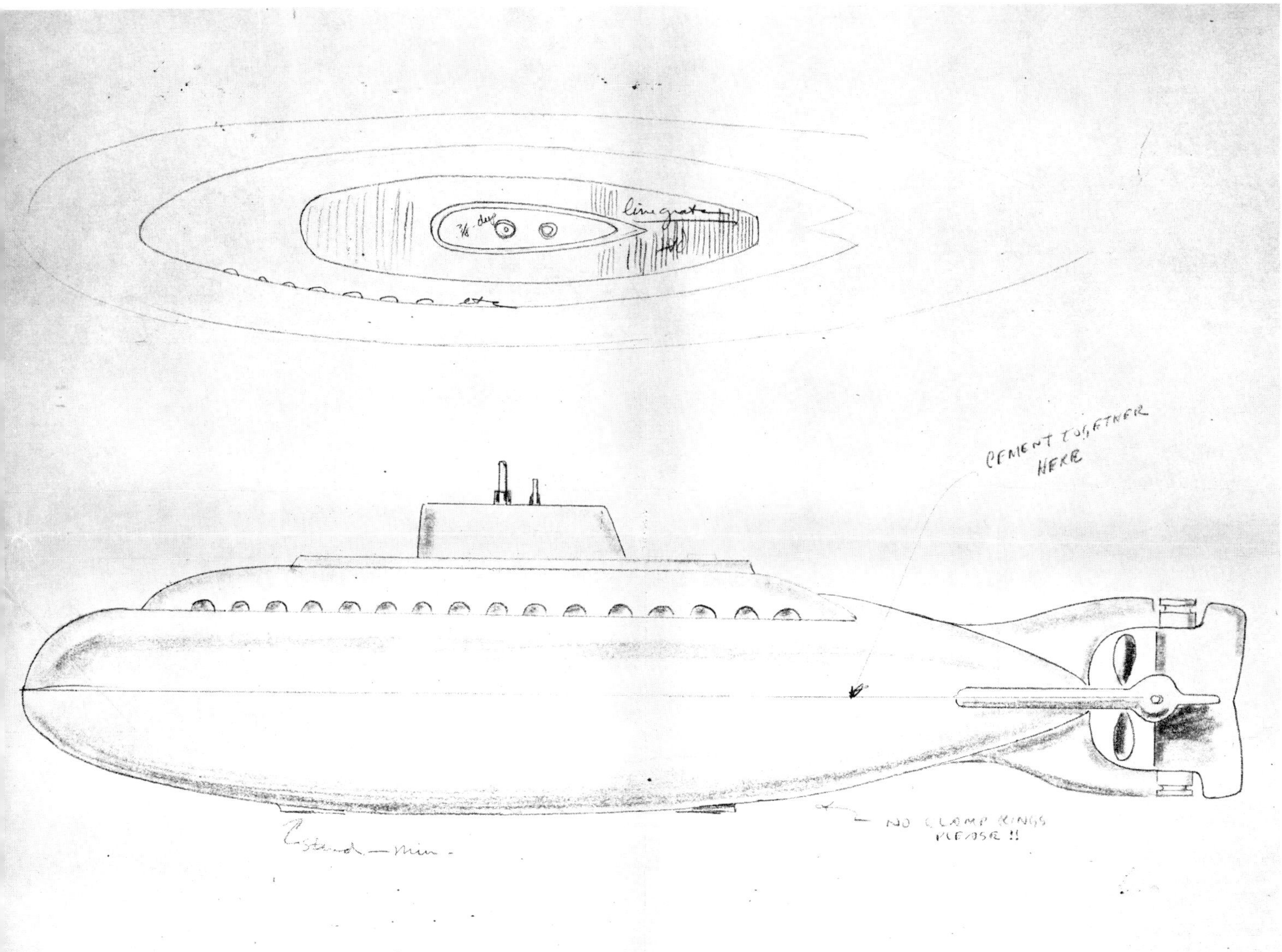

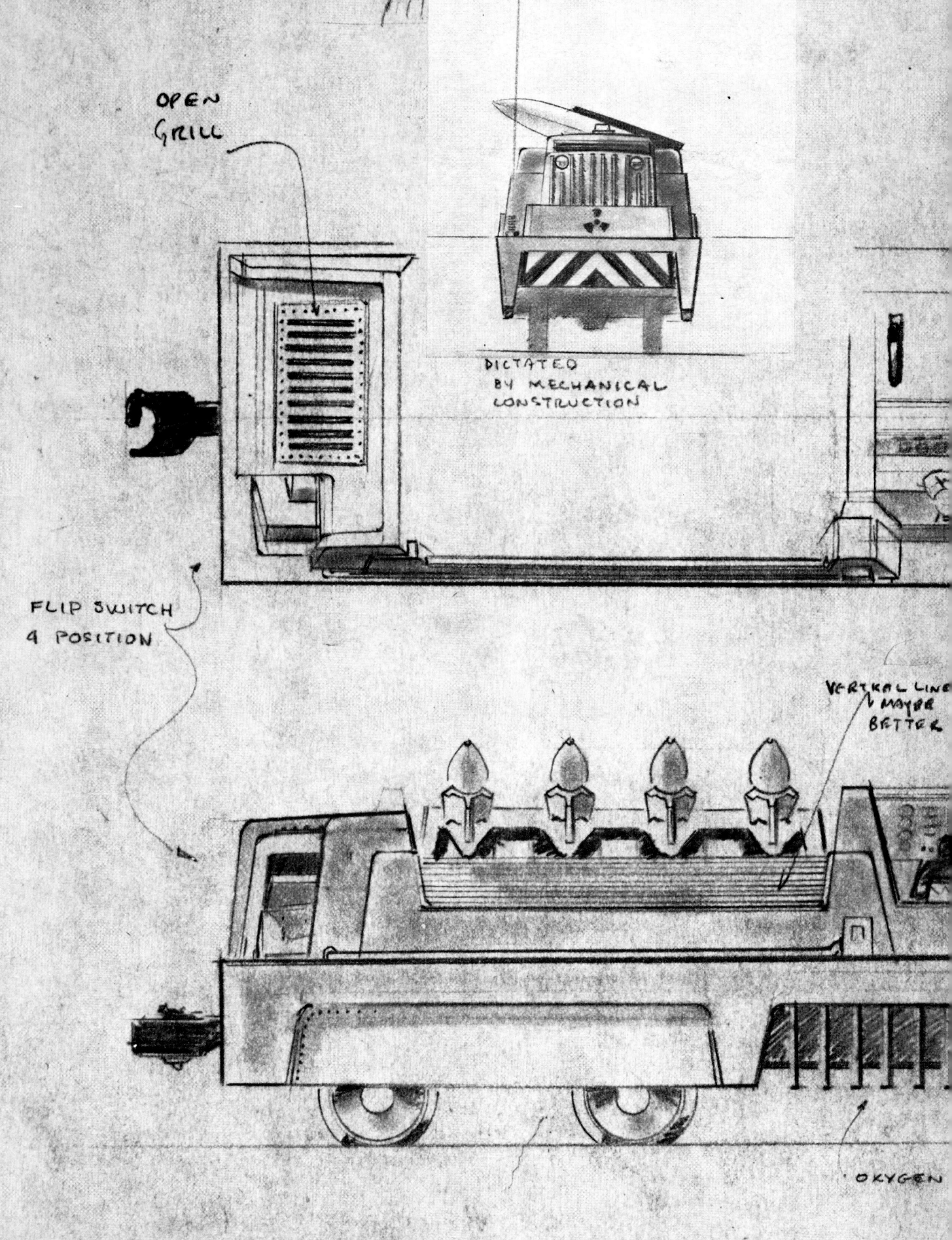

ARMY STD
MISSILE TRACKING ANT

BUMPER

DEPRESSED LOUVRES
VERTICAL LOUVRES
HEADLIGHT

CONDENSER
STEP PATTERN -
SEE FIRE CAR DECK

UHF ANTENNA

(BUBBLE COVER)
BEACON
GRILLE
SLIT WINDOWS ALL AROUND

SEE FRONT ELEVATION
DWG VDA #4-465

COOLER

DEPRESS SLIGHTLY
BOTH COVERS

NO. 4-464 ON 20 Jan 59 BY RBW

VAN DYCK ASSOCIATES

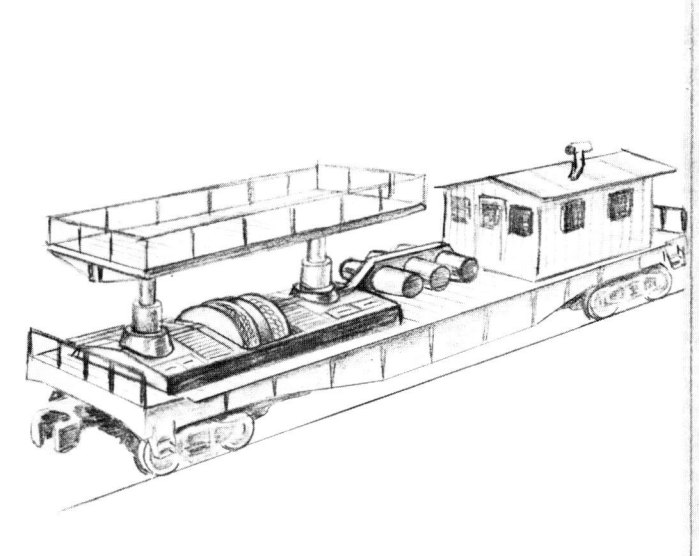
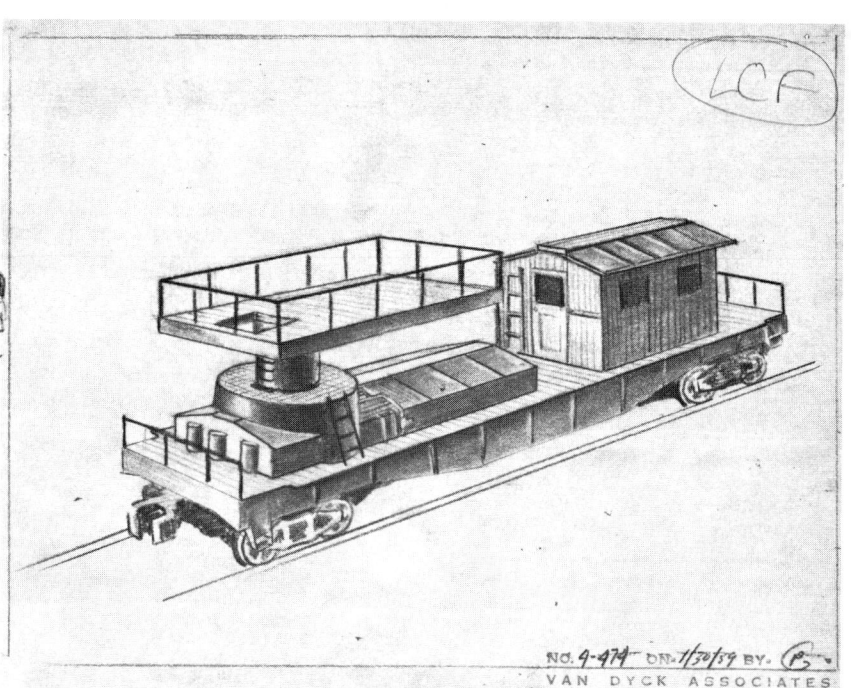
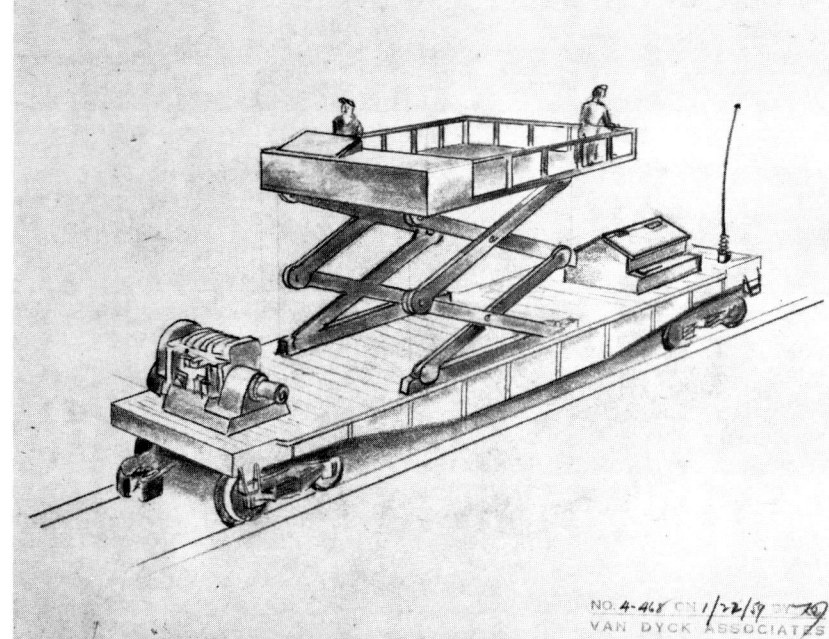
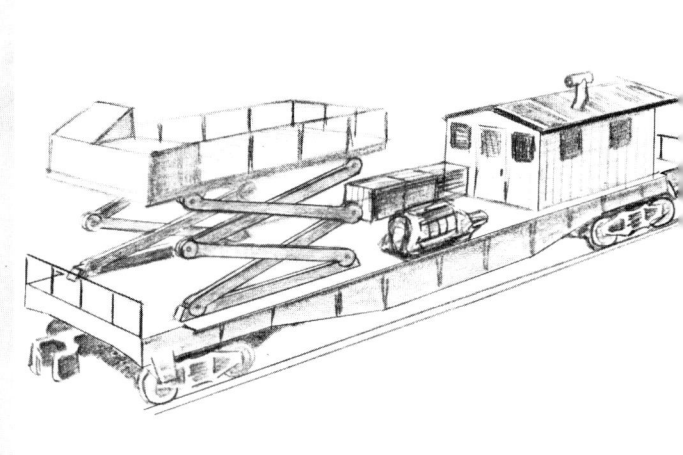
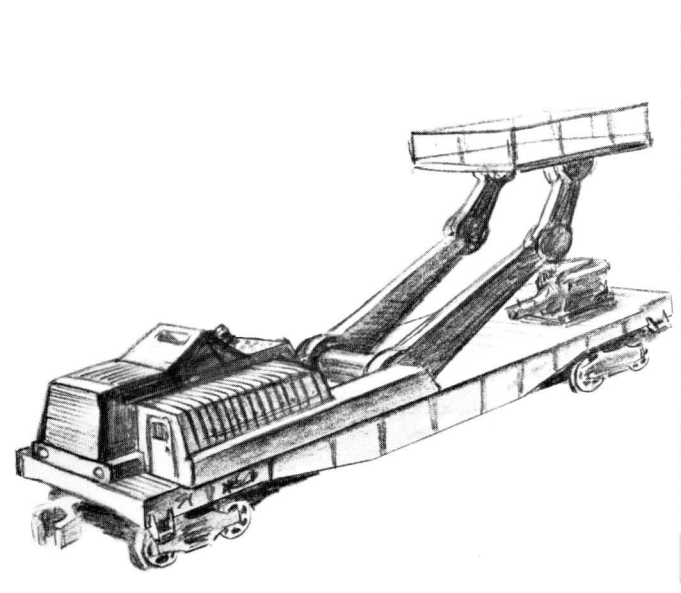

LCP
TOWER-GARAGE FOR TRUCK
USE ONLY ONE RAMP
NO. 525 ON 8-5-59 BY: JC
VAN DYCK ASSOCIATES

LCP
NO. 523 ON 8-5-59 BY: J C.
VAN DYCK ASSOCIATES

PLATFORM LOWERS
AND BRINGS
NO. 524 ON 8-5-59 BY: JC
VAN DYCK ASSOCIATES

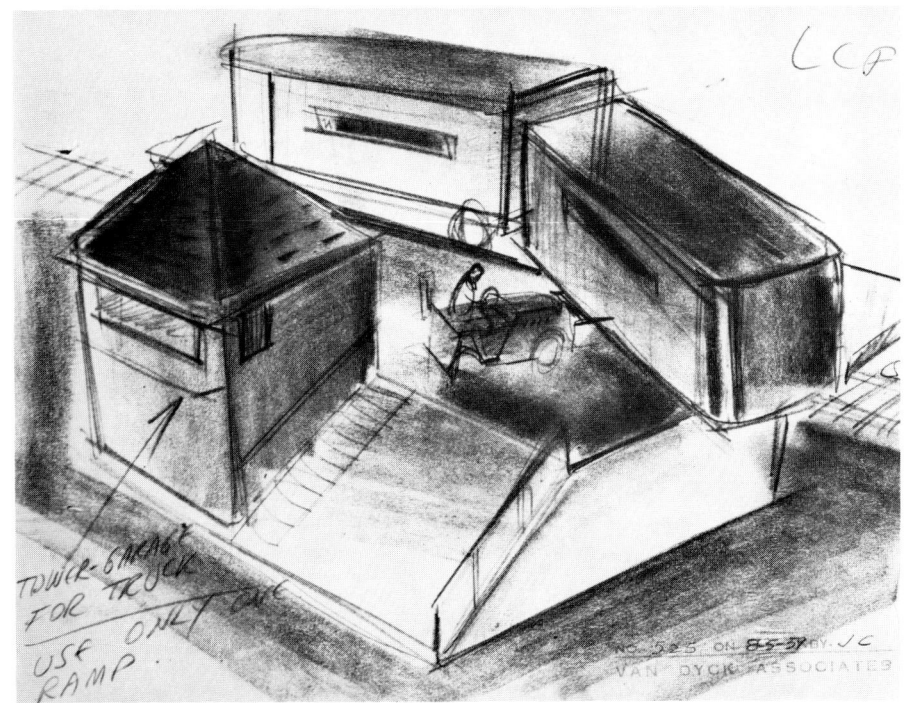

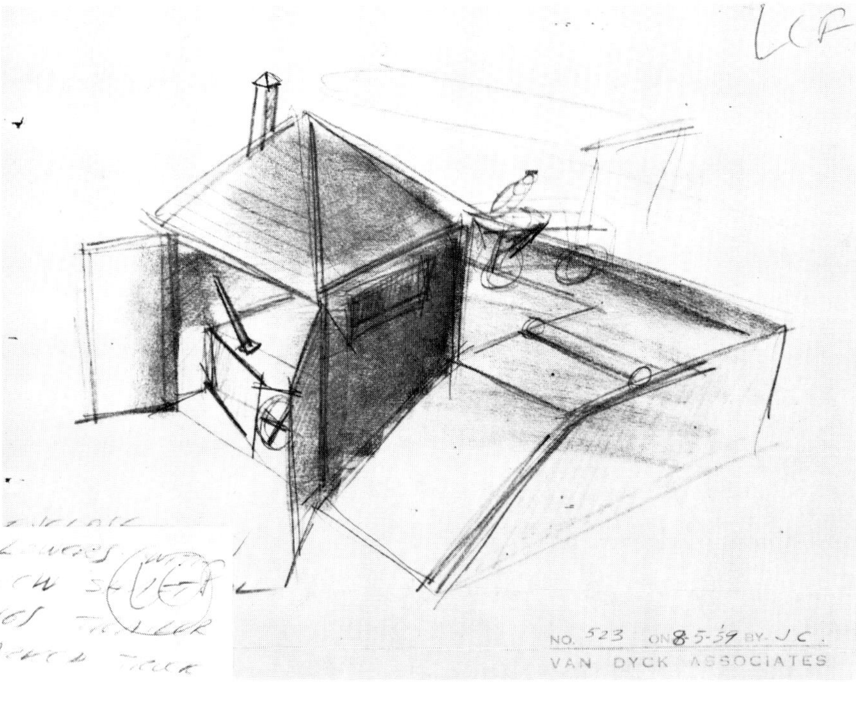

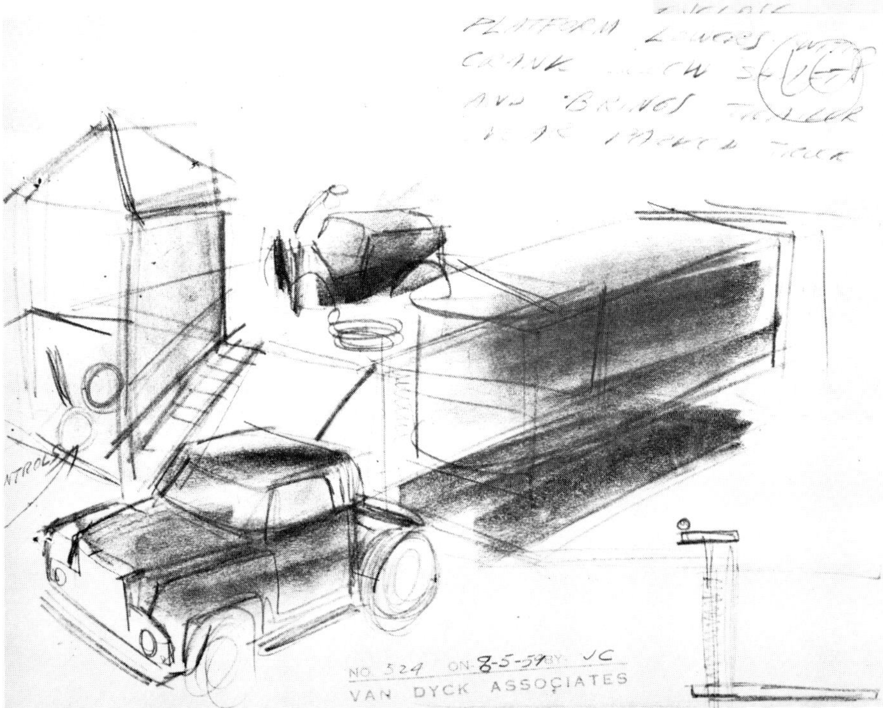

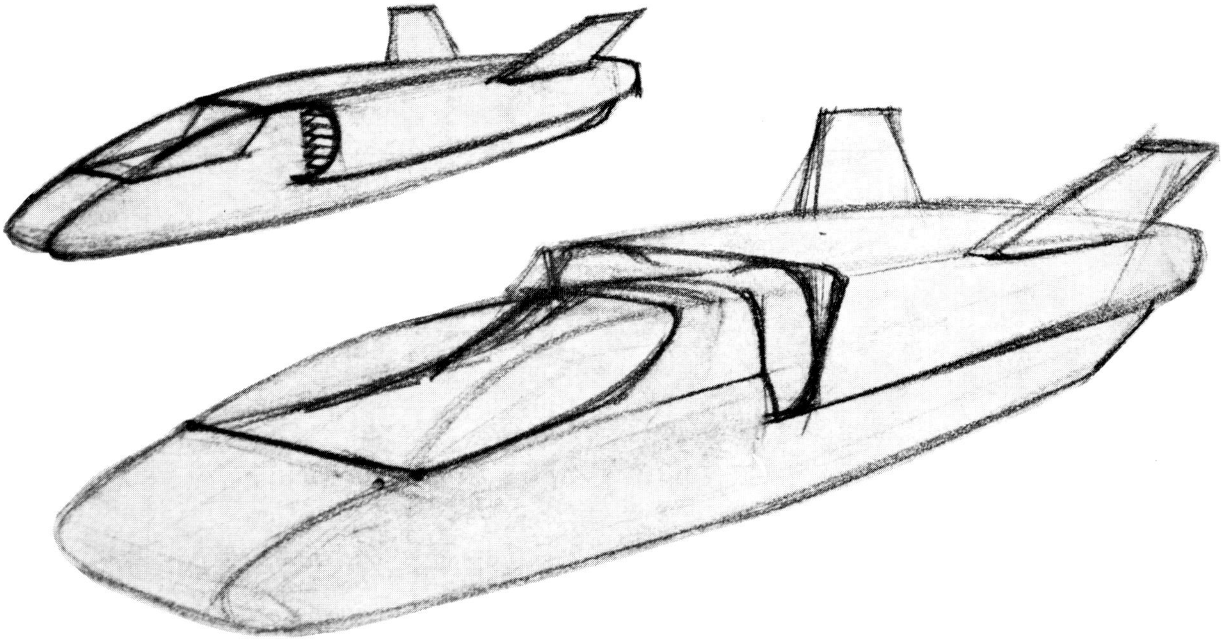

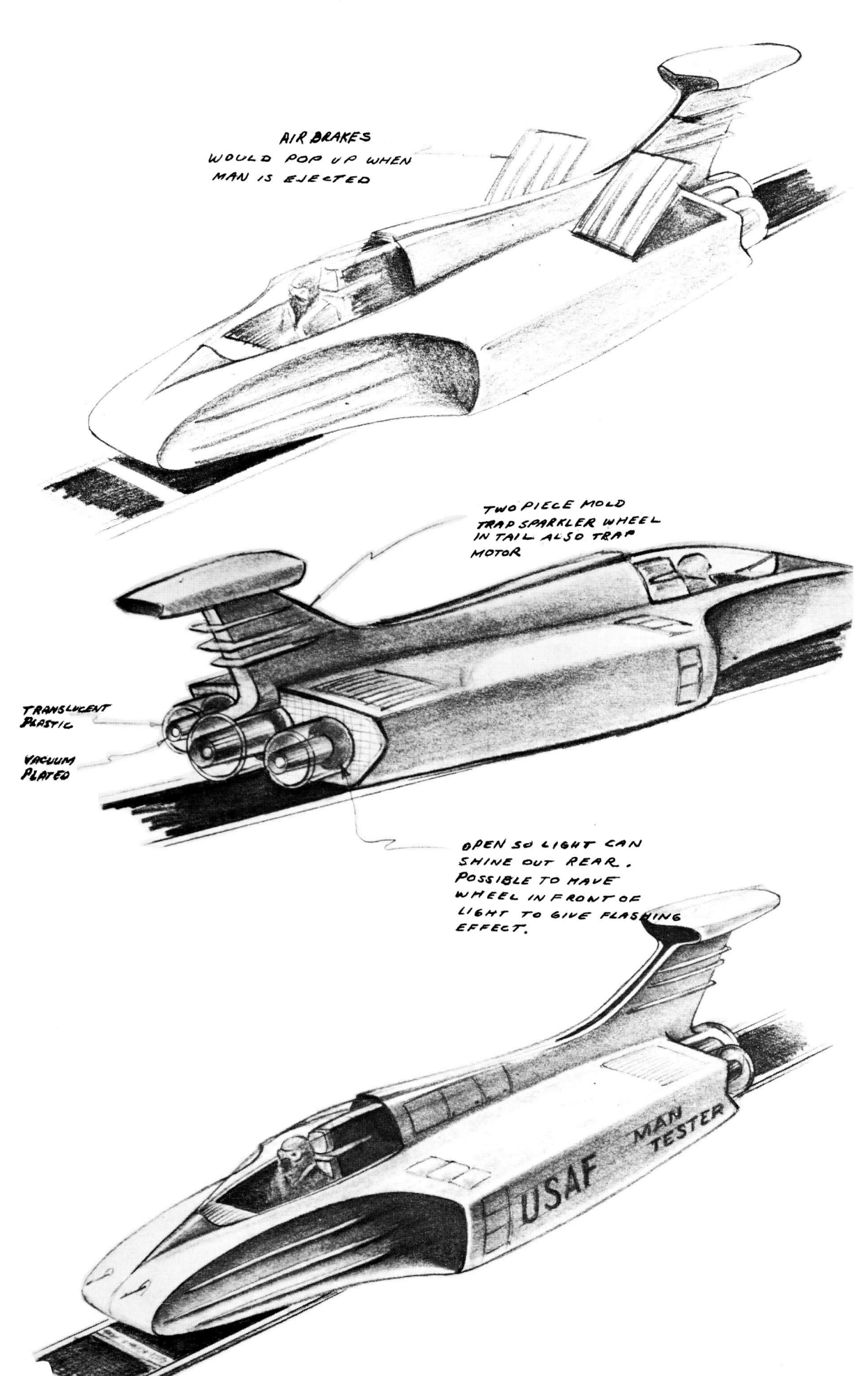

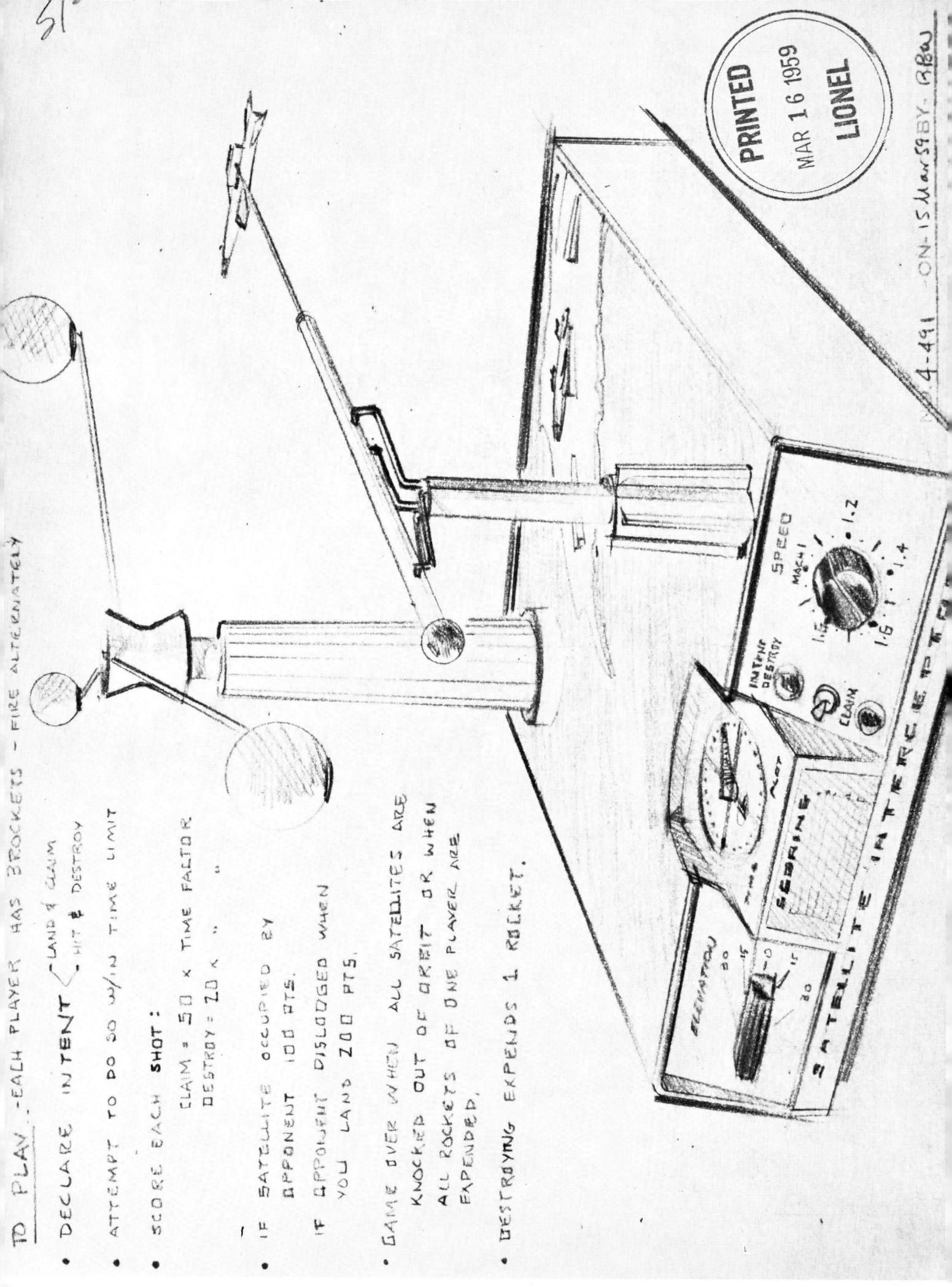

Additional Information

The *Toy Train Revue* video magazine is devoted to every aspect of toy trains. Each show is a snappy 60 minutes of lay-outs, collections, interviews, product reviews, operating tips, and factory tours – a great mix of toy train action, how-tos, and commentary.

Produced by well known toy train video producer, Tom McComas. The *Toy Train Revue* video magazine is both entertaining and informative. It may be purchased by subscription or individually, as each issue is released.
To order, call 1-800-892-2822

The *Toy Train Revue Journal* is a market report, tip sheet, and price guide all rolled into one quarterly magazine – the essential companion for the toy train collector and operator.

Our hobby has changed dramatically over the past few years and not all the changes have been for the good. Unscrupulous practices like selling fakes and reproductions as originals are costing innocent collectors thousands of dollars. The *Toy Train Revue Journal* addresses these issues and others which are crucial to the growth of the hobby.

The *TTRJ* also contains articles on collecting and operating toy trains, what's hot and what's not, and price guide updates. It is current, relevant, and necessary, ideal for both the beginner and seasoned collector.
To order, call 1-800-892-2822.

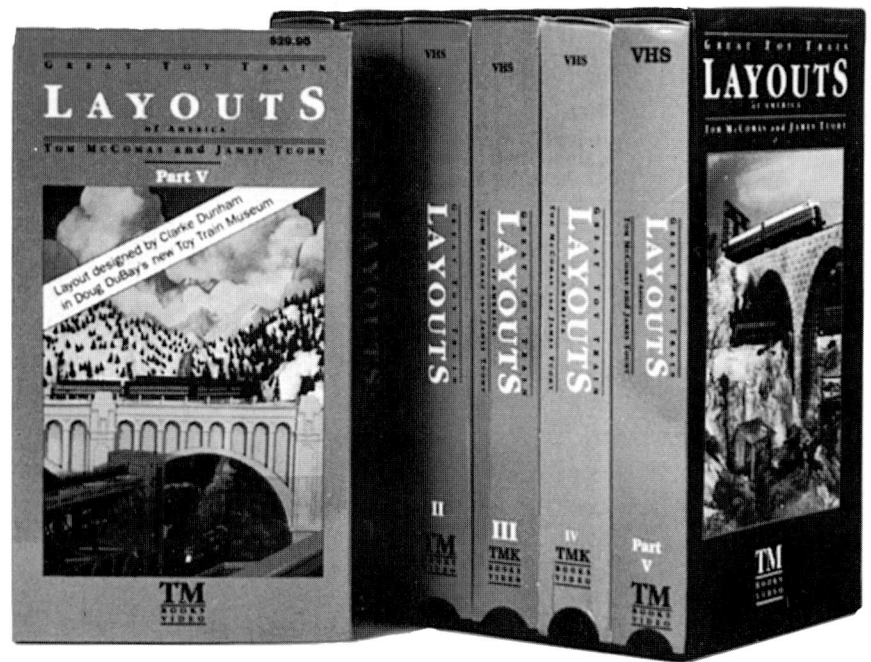

This six-part video series is an in-depth study of the most elaborate model train layouts in America. Almost six hours of action plus interviews with the layout builders. Trains and accessories of every era and almost every manufacturer. Each 45 to 55 minute show is filled with tips and hints and insights on how the experts build layouts.

Part two was chosen by *People Magazine* as one of the ten best videos of the year. If you are thinking about building a layout, or just enjoy good stories about toy trains and the people who love them, this series is a must.
To order call 1-800-892-2822.

A delightful and innovative video. Thirty minutes of toy trains, real trains, real animals, kids singing, rockets to the moon, fireworks – even a brief appeal for environmental awareness. Fast-paced action that will keep your kids (and older kids, too) enchanted time and time again.

This video is a marvelous way to introduce your kids to the fun and excitement of toy trains. They will laugh, they will learn and they will want to watch it again.

I Love Toy Trains replaced *Thomas The Tank* as my kids favorite video. Best babysitter in town."
Michael Salnick, Palm Beach, Fla.
To order, call 1-800-892-2822

**For free TM catalog, call:
1-800-892-2822**